Happy Money
Happy Life

Happy Money
Happy Life

A Multidimensional Approach to Health, Wealth, and Financial Freedom

Jason Vitug

WILEY

Published by John Wiley & Sons, Inc., Hoboken, New Jersey.
Published simultaneously in Canada.

For general information on our other products and services or for technical support, please contact our Customer Care Department within the United States at (800) 762-2974, outside the United States at (317) 572-3993 or fax (317) 572-4002.

Wiley also publishes its books in a variety of electronic formats. Some content that appears in print may not be available in electronic formats. For more information about Wiley products, visit our web site at www.wiley.com.

Library of Congress Cataloging-in-Publication Data is available:

ISBN 9781394171262 (Hardback)
ISBN 9781394171279 (ePDF)
ISBN 9781394171286 (ePUB)

Cover Design: Paul Mccarthy
Cover Art: © Jason Vitug

SKY10041261_011323

To my family and friends, the wealth I value most.

Contents

Preface: Better Luck Next Life

I was shaking my head before I uttered, "Impossible."

"You're burnt out," my doctor blurted, with his eyes solely fixed on an iPad.

How could I be burnt out from doing work I really loved? Okay, I've been on the road for almost two years, but I enjoyed it. Sure, I have been tired during the day and restless at night. The headaches come, but they do go away eventually. The physical aches that often forced me to cancel meetings, I suppose, didn't happen all that often. And truthfully, I thought it was kind of funny that I needed a nap in the middle of conversations with friends. I was unable to keep my eyes open.

"There has to be something else going on."

His eyes now fixed on me with furrowed brows, he says, "The tests are negative. Based on the symptoms you've shared, I'd say stress and possibly adrenal fatigue, but that's not a real diagnosis."

I left the doctor's office in shock. I was not shocked that I was stressed, but I was shocked that I'd been in this situation before. The mental stress, the emotional rollercoaster, the weight of financial responsibilities, and the workload—enjoyable or not—took a toll on my health.

Something was wrong. But I've mastered the skill of mental gymnastics. My hair was thinning and falling out, but maybe it's just genetics. I easily covered the rash on my chest—out of sight, out of mind. And the dark circles and bags under my eyes I could triumphantly explain as a sign of someone working hard for their dreams. Rather than do what I needed to do, I justified doing the opposite—to get things done. My body, however, had other plans; how I felt inside was now making an appearance outside.

You'd think I'd slow down. Instead, I made the ill-considered decision to keep going. Why? As a recently successful speaker and bestselling author, I was in high demand, and this was a once-in-a-lifetime opportunity. Hashtag YOLO, am I right?

When I wrote *You Only Live Once*, I shared the knowledge that time is short but can also be quite long. Within the book, I stated that the goal was to find the balance of living well today while financially planning for a better tomorrow. Time was an asset to live our dream life in this lifetime. And I shared parts of my story: I didn't grow up with much but had my essentials covered. I worked through college, made financial mistakes, ascended the corporate ladder, earned good money, and retired 40 years early. Truth be told, I didn't plan on retiring—it was more of a break. A tightly held secret of a mental break. Fortunately, my finances enabled me to take time off—a sabbatical year—in the middle of my career.

"Are you serious?" my brother asked at the time.

My parents thought I was going mad. Friends were questioning my decision in professional terms. And some coworkers were heard whispering, "He must be rich." I wasn't rich, but I was financially secure. I did plan to return to corporate America. But walking on the nontraditional path, the world offers enticing challenges and unique opportunities. My life wouldn't be the same.

In my case, I found myself as an accidental entrepreneur with a growing platform and an actionable process. I shared my story and championed my purpose. My message resonated with thousands of people. The framework helped many achieve financial and life goals. It seemed I had found my way.

But behind the success, I was struggling mentally and emotionally. The stress of entrepreneurship led to exhaustion. Dealing with the health issues of loved ones and my own took its toll. They had a "real" diagnosis, but I *only* had symptoms. I also never fully grieved the loss of a good friend. I pushed forward instead of pausing. And I continued to struggle with the intimacy of relationships and suppressed childhood traumas. The psychological weight of it all began affecting my physical health, which impacted my ability to earn income and began hurting my financial well-being. All that stress led me to withdraw socially. And as time passed, I started wondering which came first, the mental struggles or the financial issues. I didn't know where to begin or how to fix the messiness.

My phone rang. I got a call from my finance guy. The person I hired and entrusted with my money said he made some very bad decisions. Without hesitation, I let him go and used my skill at mental gymnastics to fool myself that it wasn't a big deal: I could fix the problem. At that time, I didn't understand the extent of my growing financial crisis.

I got another phone call. It was the hospital letting me know my mom was admitted after passing out at work. My mother has health issues related to chronic stress, but this time it was different. Something else was going on. To be with my mom, I shortened a work event in Tennessee. And while she was still in the emergency room, my dad also ended up in the ER. So, there I was, visiting two hospital beds. I was being visibly strong for my parents and running my growing business. In reality, I was just trying to keep it all together.

And in keeping with Murphy's Law, I received yet another phone call, this time about a legal issue. The person angrily stated they'd tried reaching me multiple times. The woman on the other end of the call was vocally agitated. She wanted me to pay up. But as someone who knows a thing or two about finance, I knew my legal rights and asked for more details. She didn't respond well to my request and hung up. I don't recall the specific financial details, but I remember how this person made me feel. It's seared into my memory. In her words, I was incompetent, useless, and a low-life.

Eventually, I was served a court summons: I was being sued. I tried a reasonable option to make right what my finance person did wrong but to no avail. That led me to seek advice from the alphabet soup of financial professionals: a certified public accountant (CPA), a certified financial planner (CFP®), accredited financial counselors (AFC®), and two attorneys. I created a money team to help me make one of the biggest financial decisions ever.

I started this journey as a financially secure early retiree and ended up as a bankrupted entrepreneur.

Better luck next life, am I right?

We all have mental challenges and emotional baggage. It's often easier to deal with them when we have the financial means or to ignore them by purchasing stuff or taking a vacation (aka taking a break from our stressful life). And when we can't afford these things, we emphasize that the lack of money prevents us from feeling happy.

What I've learned is how we're not spending money happily. Sure, you can spend your money as you wish on anything: it's your money. But, spending money to affect your overall well-being leads to long-term satisfaction rather than short-term gratification.

I was left pondering a question: money can solve money problems, but how can money solve life problems?

Getting better with money meant improving my financial health. With better financial means, I lessened my stress levels, but it didn't mean I was living a happy life. I knew how to affect my mood through purchases (goods or experiences), but I hadn't improved my overall well-being.

I kept searching for the answer and came to a realization: it's essential to improve financial health because it gives us the resources to work on life problems.

In 2018, while enjoying a cup of coffee on the balcony of my Airbnb in Positano, Italy, I had an epiphany—it was all connected. Everything. My financial, mental, and physical health were all connected. My research led me to the eight wellness dimensions: intellectual, physical, emotional, spiritual, financial, environmental, occupational, and social health.

After understanding the different wellness dimensions, I realized their interconnectedness. Working on one dimension impacts another and can affect multiple areas. It gave me an idea. To improve my condition, I needed to address an area of high concern at the time—my finances. I focused on financial health, a dimension I had more knowledge in, to get the biggest impact.

My efforts to improve my financial health led to making the best financial decision for my situation. It would eventually lead to a positive ripple effect on other wellness dimensions.

But making the best financial decision wasn't easy. It tested and pushed the limits of my emotional and spiritual health. If my identity was tied to professional and financial success, then who am I? I was someone who felt broken and defeated. It was a time of so much turmoil and pain. I was deathly afraid of what other people would think and wasn't sure if I could handle any more stress.

I sought therapy and decided to take a step back—allowing myself time to process. Unfortunately, stepping away from the work that made me feel alive only left me feeling alone. I lost my sense of purpose and, with it, my spirit—my inspiration to participate in life. I felt worthless, a sham, an imposter until a good friend said, "You know who your people are when they cheer for your resurgence."

Well, this is my resurgence. The test of my resiliency against the grip of *ill*-ness to a space of *well*-ness. I am in a *happy place*. I've become more open about my struggles and how those issues affected my financial health. And how improving my financial health has elevated my overall well-being. In this journey, I'm learning my willingness to be vulnerable publicly is helping in my healing and giving others HOPE—*Hearing Other People's Experiences*.

Through all this, my belief holds true: you only live once. But you get the opportunity to have many lives in one lifetime. When one journey ends, another begins. We are allowed to make mistakes but must give ourselves space and grace to move past them. We can start anew. We can reinvent ourselves a multitude of times. We can try and fail and try again. And when we hit rock bottom, it simply means we're only left with one option—the choice to go up. I chose to get up.

If you're wondering where "better luck next life" came from, it was from a fellow blogger who attended my *You Only Live Once* book event at a financial conference in San Diego. He shared his cultural belief in reincarnation and explained that the phrase "better luck next life" is a reminder that we "get to live again and again until we get it right." So, he jokingly said I was wrong and that "we don't live just once." Well, I do know one thing for sure: we get an opportunity to live again and again until we get it right but in the span of one lifetime.

Who knew years later that four words from a stranger would be the perfect preface title to encapsulate a period of my life? I wish I remembered his name and could thank him. But if that's you and you're reading this, I want you to know I'm having better luck in my *next* life.

In the past few years, we've been through a lot. We all have experienced a time filled with loss, uncertainty, fear, and pain. Its psychological impact will be felt for years. It makes sense that mental and emotional health is a topic of importance for many. And it's a reason why I've written this book. I want to share the interconnection of financial health with overall well-being to guide you to a healthy and happier version of yourself.

Surprisingly, with all the economic uncertainty, my toughest financial decision better prepared me for the pandemic. I was mentally stronger, doing financially well, and had a reorganized business positioned at the forefront of financial health. And in the loneliness of quarantine, I found a renewed sense of purpose and vigor to serve it.

During the quarantine, my scheduled speaking gigs were postponed indefinitely, so I used my "free" time to address an area I had neglected for far too long—my physical health. As a self-described bad cook, I learned to cook healthy using meal kit delivery services. And after years of on- and- off practice, I completed my 200-hour yoga teacher certification and finally understood yoga—a connection of mind, body, and spirit. I was also introduced to the power of breathwork (and got certified, too), which is helping me respond to my thoughts and feelings.

As the pandemic days turned to months, I read many books to understand myself, others, and the world and my place in it. I became *that* dog person who must hold the world record for dog photos on a smartphone and gained a deeper understanding of emotional intelligence.

In many ways, I'm living a different life within the same lifetime.

Some people, believing I've made an unforgivable financial decision, will ask why they or anyone else should listen to me. As my money team would collectively say, some of the biggest voices in personal finance and business have no issue using their legal right to asset protection. And my attorney would add, "it just makes them more relatable."

I'm unsure if they're more relatable but they're possibly more like real people. I'm a real person who's faced personal struggles and financial challenges but still holding onto hope and big dreams. I know many people facing a multitude of wellness issues and holding onto hope and big dreams. Maybe you're one of them, and that's why this book is in your hands.

In my "previous life," I didn't know how to share these stories of mental health and financial issues. Fortunately, in living my next life, sharing these stories of health and wealth is the basis of *Happy Money Happy Life*.

Perhaps you'll relate to my story or be repelled by it. But maybe, just maybe, you'll come to learn how someone who seemed to have it all together and then lost it all was able to bounce back healthier, wealthier, and happier.

A Poetic Introduction

Happy money truths.
You will save.
You will invest.
You will pay off debt.
You will spend a little less.
And make a bit more.
But You will live.
Not just alive.
Willing
and Living.
A happy life.
Less money worries.
And more life stories.

Introduction

You want to be happy.

I believe you *deserve* to be happy, so I've written this book for you. If you've picked up this book and believe money can help you be happier, you're in for a treat. And if you believe money can't buy happiness but are open to new ideas, this book is most definitely for you too.

I wrote this book because I discovered a fundamental truth—*money isn't everything, but it impacts most things.*

And as in most things, money affects how you think and feel about yourself and how you relate to others, and it impacts your experiences at home, at work, and in society.

Money affects your happiness.

Whether you agree or disagree that money can lead to a happy life, we've built a society that runs on money. And those who learn to master it gain the advantage of choosing happiness.

"But, money can't buy happiness," people have said repeatedly. I believe this is said in an effort for some to keep "the truth" a secret. The people who understand money's effect on happiness often earn more and create wealth, while those living without "the truth" struggle to make ends meet.

Money can buy happiness because it allows you to afford the necessities of life, such as housing, food, clothing, and medicine. And when you're able to pay for the essentials and some luxuries too, it becomes easier to choose happiness.

While money can buy happiness, money *isn't* happiness.

It's crucial to understand the difference. Your purpose in life is not to chase, earn, and hoard money. It's a resource to be used. When used according to a set of principles (you'll learn in this book), it enables you to serve a greater good, your life's purpose.

You need to be good with money to have a happy life in this world. That doesn't mean you need to earn the most, have the most, or even be a millionaire (although I will share how to do just that). This book approaches money as your tool; as such, you'll need to learn what it is, how to handle it, and where to use it to achieve your goals.

I will challenge your beliefs about money and its tangible and intangible qualities, and provide you with a practical and systematic approach. You will learn to shift your thinking to enable money to flow into your life, so you can direct the outward flow to areas that support your happiness and well-being.

But I've also learned why so many, including myself, have difficulty allowing money to flow and why we've been messy with our finances. The financial messiness fosters a lot of stress. It takes a toll on our mental and emotional well-being, often manifesting itself in physical ailments. And if that wasn't enough, being a financial mess can affect our experiences, relationships, work satisfaction, and living conditions.

Could you reach financial milestones and still be unhappy? Absolutely.

Is it possible you are overspending to buy happiness? Possibly.

Are you not happy because of your finances, or are your finances a result of your unhappiness? The goal of this book is to help you connect the dots.

In short, I'm here to share how money affects other parts of your life—the mental, emotional, physical, spiritual, social, occupational, and environmental— and how those parts have an inverse effect on your financial health.

MY HAPPY MESSAGES

My attempt isn't to explain everything and overwhelm you. I aim to share what I believe are the simplest and most effective ways to live financially well and have a happy life. The key themes throughout the book include:

- Happiness varies for everyone because *your* needs are different.
- You *can* choose to be happy.
- Your money *buys* happiness by impacting health and wellness.

FINANCIAL ISOLATION

During the pandemic isolation period, many had realizations about their financial health. People with money and good jobs found flexibility and comfort amidst the uncertainty. Conversely, other people experienced financial vulnerability, heightened mental stress, and emotional exhaustion. And some who practiced extreme frugality and avoided dining out with friends began feeling the effects of social isolation on their well-being.

Many of these people made a good income, saved, and invested, while others were experiencing financial shortcomings. But all were seeking more than dollars and cents. They wanted joy and happiness.

If you're connecting the dots, you're on the verge of a major shift with money that leads to holistic well-being. Within these pages, you'll learn how money affects financial health and impacts your thoughts and feelings, physical condition, the spirit within, social life, home comforts, and work satisfaction.

We've been told that our financial issues can lead to mental and emotional distress. But the reverse is true too. Our mental and emotional health often impacts our finances and affects how we save, spend, and invest money. This is why I've written this book, to offer you a better way to master finances to reach your goals and improve your well-being.

Ask yourself, *What's the **value** of mental and emotional well-being? What **price** will you pay for better physical health? What's the **cost** of choosing meaningful work? What's the **return** on living in a nice home and better neighborhood? Can you **afford** not to have friends? What's your **worth** without work and purpose?*

As you can see (and perhaps already know), money weaves itself into every aspect of our lives. Yet, we don't think of money in that way, and we haven't been taught how to manage money for happiness, satisfaction, and well-being.

Before starting this journey, I want you to reflect on where you are today. Own your starting point whether you're doing well or struggling a bit. It doesn't matter how you start, but where you end up. The place you end up in will largely be attributed to the knowledge, work, and determination to keep moving forward.

Let's move forward.

HOW TO USE THIS BOOK

The book has three parts and is written like a cohesively intertwined trilogy. This was done to show a progressive connection. You'll gain a high-level view of happiness and practical steps to master money. Book I is on happiness, Book II is on life, and Book III is on money.

I wrote this book with an intentional flow and conclusion, but it was written to allow you to skip around and read specific chapters as often as necessary. Do you want to find meaningful work? Go to Chapter 6. Do you want to learn about mental health? Go to Chapter 7. Do you want to find your purpose? Flip to Chapter 12. Do you want to invest for financial independence? Turn to Chapter 24.

However, I suggest reading the entire book so you know what it can offer you. And you have my permission (okay, it's your book so permit yourself) to mark it up, highlight paragraphs, underline sentences, and circle words. Feel free to write your thoughts on the edges. Make notes about what makes sense or sparked more questions. Don't be afraid to fold or dog-ear pages so that you can return to the sections that are most important to you. And I encourage you to get a journal or notebook for the simple exercises.

Now that's out of the way, what will *you* be learning?

Book I: In Pursuit of Happiness

In this section, you'll learn the science behind happiness in a very artful way that will inspire you to prioritize the pursuit of happiness.

In the following chapters, you'll learn how money affects your life and how to spend money to improve your well-being and experience long-term happiness.

Happiness
You can choose to be happy.
Money can buy happiness, but money *isn't* happiness.
Money buys happiness by impacting health and wellness.
Improve your well-being and experience long-term happiness.

Book II: Happy Life

In this section, you'll learn about the eight happy dimensions. You'll understand the interconnectedness and how money affects each dimension.

Happy Life You only live once; make it a happy life.	
Happy Money (Financial)	Living financially free.
Happy Work (Occupational)	Rewire; don't retire.
Happy Mind (Mental)	Invest in yourself and learn continually.
Happy Heart (Emotional)	Memories appreciate; stuff depreciates.
Happy Body (Physical)	Be kind to your body; it's priceless.
Happy Social (Social)	Connections are your lifeline.
Happy Space (Environmental)	Free your space and yourself.
Happy Spirit (Spiritual)	Serve a purpose, not a purchase.

Book III: Happy Money

In this section, you'll learn strategies and tactics to improve your finances to reach your goals.

Part 1: Shift your **money beliefs** to get what you really want.
Part 2: Assess your **money vitals** to improve your financial health.
Part 3: Start your **money journey** to reach financial freedom.

Are you ready? Let's get started on your journey to Happy Money Happy Life.

BOOK I

In Pursuit of Happiness

Happiness is the meaning and the purpose of life, the whole aim, and end of human existence.

—Aristotle

Life's too short to pursue anything else than happiness.

"Is this what retirement means?" she asked, staring directly into my eyes.

My mom was sitting at the examination table. We've been to multiple doctors. She's undergone multiple tests. It was the confirmation of what we already knew to be a fact. But hearing the words left an indelible mark.

"You have Parkinson's," the doctor said.

My mom started crying. I couldn't hold back my tears. I walked over and grabbed her hands. Pulling me closer, she dropped her head onto my chest, sobbing. I wrapped my arms around her trembling body and said, "Everything will be okay."

I wasn't quite sure if everything would be okay. But I needed to say something to alleviate the suffering my mom was experiencing.

On her commute to work, she had started feeling her left leg shaking from time to time. As months passed, the shaking moved to her arm. And then the muscle stiffness began. A neurologist said we could slow down the progression through medication and exercises. I asked

1

him if there was anything else that could be done. He looked at my mom and asked, "What do you enjoy doing?"

Upon hearing the question, she started crying. It had been like this for quite some time. When another doctor asked her, "What are your hobbies and passions?" My mom paused for a minute and said, "I don't know."

My mom has spent most of her life working to earn a living. She's been the breadwinner for years and managed the household finances. I never saw her spend money on herself. But my parents did spend money on a lot of things. One day, as we packed their belongings for their retirement move, she said, "I want to be happy." I wasn't quite sure if sifting through stuff made her reflect on past purchases or her life.

We spend most of our lives exchanging our time for a paycheck. At first, to afford the necessities of life, then we spend more just to escape the lifestyle we've mindlessly created. We're buying things to make us happy, even though we know it doesn't last long. So we continue working to earn money to keep buying. We live to work to spend. At the same time, we hope that one day we can live life in retirement.

I've learned one thing about life: nothing is guaranteed. I'm sure you've learned that lesson too. We've all lived through massive changes from 9/11 to the Great Recession to the pandemic. And whether the changes are personal or global, I'm reminded that most things are out of our control, but some things are ours to control, like *choosing happiness*.

My financial health gives me choices. It allows me to be there for my parents. I've spent the past few years as a de facto caretaker for them. I've shared with friends: if I can't help my parents, why am I working so hard? What kind of life am I designing?

I have the financial means. I work for myself. I don't have to report to an office, and I can pick and choose the work I do. My boss might sometimes be demanding, but I've learned to give myself space and grace. It wasn't always like this. I had to make better decisions to make this life possible.

My pursuit of happiness meant pursuing wellness. I realized it wasn't about chasing the emotion. It meant taking care of the different aspects of myself to be prepared for opportunities and to become stronger in difficult times. There have been many difficult times. And even in those difficulties, I found happiness.

Happiness is personal. It's as personal as love. It's a universal emotion we get to have, but how we describe it varies from person to person. I've learned that chasing happiness and buying stuff—believing stuff *is* happiness—just leaves us dissatisfied, unhappy, and unwell. There is a better way to pursue happiness in life.

The phrase "the pursuit of happiness" are words we know well. It's enshrined in the Declaration of Independence. When I ask people to define happiness, the responses always start with "for me, happiness is ...." And that's because it's personalized. It's quite possible that was the intention of the phrase, "life, liberty and the pursuit of _____ (fill in the blank).

What is happiness to you? Can you define it? Articulate it? Do you feel happy as you describe it?

Happiness is such a nebulous emotion. You can be happy with a stranger's kind gesture and happy in the arms of a lover. You can be happy reading a book and happy working on a project. You can be happy exploring the world and happy sitting on the couch. You can be happy when others are sad. And you can be suffering while others are happy.

We're unhappy because we're suffering in small and big ways. People are suffering because they can't afford medicine. People are suffering because of cheating spouses. People are suffering because of crime. People suffer from emotional turmoil, loneliness, physical pain, debt, and the weather.

We all want to be happy as an antidote to suffering. Perhaps, we could say we're "in pursuit of less suffering."

How do you want to suffer less?

I've met thousands of people in my work and had many personal conversations. It is no longer surprising that we talk about life and happiness, not merely money and investments.

"Life is short, but life can be long too," I'd say. "We still have time for more happiness."

"You can't be happy all the time," yells a heckler. "You're just fooling yourself."

I was giving a talk about money and happiness when I was interrupted. It was such a negative take on what seemed like an optimistic pursuit. I know I can't be happy all the time. It's an emotion. Emotions come and go.

"If I can't be happy all the time, then it's safe to assume I can't be sad all the time too?" I asked.

He didn't respond. I noticed that his mind was making a connection.

Many people do face life challenges and believe a way to happiness is more money. It can be. However, people who believe money *is* happiness pursue it endlessly, never finding fulfillment. The pursuit of money took them away from connections, meaning, and wellness. It left them broken, defeated, and lonely.

And the few who pursued big dreams, while broke and financially struggling, found satisfaction and wealth. They were driven by something else—a sense of purpose.

But money does give us more options to pursue a different path. Many others shared their pursuit of leaving toxic jobs, escaping crime-ridden neighborhoods, and abusive relationships. They've told me their stories of childhood trauma, mental health issues, and physical illnesses. And many were able to heal, escape, and start anew because money, in one way or another, offered them options.

The people with these life challenges didn't believe more money would make them happy in their situations. They saw money as a tool to get them out.

Money gives people options, but it's the choices that are made that lead to happiness.

I've learned in the past few years that if I experience sadness because of situations, I also experience happiness based on situations. It was imperative for me to understand what situations fostered more happiness.

I discovered the growing trend in happiness research through positive psychology. Previous research has focused mostly on negative emotions rather than positive ones. But I simply didn't want to avoid sadness. I wanted to be happier. My curiosity led me to pursue an artful nonscientific study of happiness.

What does happiness mean to you?

CHAPTER 1

The Artful Nonscience of Happiness

'Ve held hundreds of events in 44 states across the United States. I've met thousands of people from all walks of life in different life situations and circumstances. The differences in lived experiences are unmistakable, but one similarity is unquestionable: we all want to be happy.

"Is there something more?" a voice emerged from the crowded bar.

Over pizza and beer, I shared my story of financial struggles and professional success.

"Who said that?"

I scanned the room to see who shouted the question: a 21-year-old Mizzou college student with a perplexed look stood up.

"Was there anything else going on to leave a good-paying job you said you loved?" he asked.

"There's much more to the story than turning my back on professional success. But to be truthful, I'm not quite ready to get into those details. I can share that money fixes money problems, but it isn't *the* answer to life problems," I replied.

Not surprisingly, many people want the intricate details of how I was a high-earning financial mess. They wanted to know what I was going through that affected my finances. Perhaps, it might be similar to their nonfinancial issue or existential crisis.

After my talks, I get an opportunity to have deeper conversations with people who privately share their mental, emotional, physical, and professional issues affecting their path to financial wellness. Some people have used retail therapy to deal with mental and emotional suffering. But doing so led to overspending and financial instability, which added to their psychological distress. I've heard stories of determined individuals accumulating wealth to provide a good life for their families. Unfortunately, the same determination toward financial success took them away from what they said was important—a good time with their family.

These very people who showed vulnerability gave me the strength to be vulnerable, too. I've become more open about how I was a high-earning financial mess. Not because I didn't understand finance but because my mental stresses, emotional immaturity, professional perfectionism, and spiritual misguidance impacted my finances. And how all of it impacted my happiness.

"How can we be happier?" he asked.

"Perhaps, if I had the answer, I'd be on a hammock at the beach on a remote island in the Pacific," I joked.

Happiness isn't a destination, though. Some mistake happiness as a product for purchase. You can't buy a ticket to happiness. It's an emotion you feel as a response to situations and environments.

But you might experience happiness visiting a happier country ranked on the United Nations' World Happiness Report.[1] In a way, you can buy a ticket for an experience, but you'll still have the nagging question: how can I be happy at home?

What is happiness?

There have been numerous studies and philosophical thoughts on happiness and how to have it. *Happiness* is challenging to define because it's very personal to each and every one of us. But it's also influenced by many factors that can be observed.

There is a body of research on happiness. I read the studies and will share some fascinating details, but I wanted to learn directly from others. I spoke with 100 people about happiness. I didn't conduct a research study. I listened to people's countless stories of failures and successes. People who faced insurmountable odds and triumphed. And how they find ways to choose happiness.

I discovered common traits of happy people in my artful nonscientific study.

Happier people have autonomy, are self-regulating and socially active, and have flexible and curious minds. Many didn't have hard-set rules about living life.

People shared what contributed to their happiness, which included continually learning, being physically healthy, expressing emotions, having friends, doing meaningful work, having a sense of purpose, and living in healthier environments supporting their lifestyle.

Money was a common theme: all expressed the importance of financial health. However, mindsets varied greatly. People who felt they had enough money saw it as a tool to build their dreams. They associated struggles with character building. People who felt they didn't have enough believed money was an obstacle to their happiness. They defaulted to saying that "money can't buy happiness," while prioritizing the pursuit of money.

My conversations led me to a discovery: people who said they have autonomy and a sense of control are happier.

Autonomy is the ability to act according to one's values and beliefs. People who acted based on their values and beliefs were happier. There was an alignment among their thoughts, feelings, and actions. Money was securing, not stress-inducing.

A sense of control was associated with happiness.

It's not the type of control you're thinking of. It's accepting that you don't have much control in the first place; therefore, you focus on the areas you can influence. You can't control your partner, but you can choose to communicate differently or leave the relationship. You can't control the economy, but you can control how you save and spend. You can't control how much employers pay, but you can control how to gain skills to get a better job. Having control gives a sense of calm in a chaotic and unpredictable world. People who feel powerless often can't see how much control they still have over aspects of their lives.

People are happier because they have options.

But it's about making better choices. For instance, money allows you the option to quit a toxic job, but it doesn't make the decision for you. There are plenty of unhappy workers with high incomes unable to make a choice to leave. They continue choosing options that lock them into the job.

Two conversations about choices have stuck with me. One person shared he was unhappy at work and bought a new car. Another said he was unhappy in the relationship and bought an engagement ring. Both believed buying stuff was the best option to fix the problem. In contrast, people who better understand their values make happier choices. For them, choosing happiness would mean buying their way out of the job or the relationship.

A better relationship with money contributes to happiness.

I recognized a difference among the highest-income earners who were, or weren't, happy in my nonscientific study. The happy highest-income earners used their money to improve different aspects of their lives. There's intentionality in how they spend money. It's a quality shared by others who said they were happy, regardless of income.

In contrast, people who focused on financial numbers and visual displays of wealth were less happy regardless of income. It never seemed to be enough. Even though their financial numbers or lifestyles showed otherwise.

YOUR INCOME AND HAPPINESS

A famous Princeton study by Angus Deaton and Daniel Kahneman is often cited: the relationship between happiness and income plateaus at $75,000 (roughly $90,000 given inflation). Deaton and Kahneman used "life evaluation" and "emotional well-being" to discover how income affects happiness. The study concluded "that high income buys life satisfaction but not happiness, and that low income is associated both with low life evaluation and low emotional well-being."[2]

They learned that life evaluation rises steadily with income. Emotional well-being (happiness) also rises with income, but only up to $75,000. People focused on the second part of the study, and it's been misinterpreted.

I saw a connection: mindset and emotions play a far bigger role in money and happiness.

We're doing a mental exercise when asked to evaluate our life.

I've learned that there is no income cap to "life evaluation" happiness. When you see your income rise, it's often associated with other accomplishments. You are making more because you graduated college, got a promotion, started a business, and so on. Evaluating life in the context of money and accomplishment would make you feel happier. It's because you associate your hard work and effort with increased income.

We're doing an emotional assessment when asked about dealing with pain.

How much income do you need to feel happy about a medical diagnosis, a lost loved one, or divorce? In my artful interpretation, having the income to cover expenses helps deal with the financial aspect of the pain, but a higher income isn't going to make the pain go away. However, having higher incomes does allow for a broader set of emotions by reducing the financial stress associated with life circumstances.

Another study by a University of Pennsylvania Wharton researcher found that happiness rises above the $75,000 a year income threshold.[3] Matthew Killingsworth's study suggests that "higher incomes may still have potential to improve people's day-to-day well-being." Basically, making more money supports happiness through wellness activities.

Both the Princeton and Wharton studies found people experience more stress as they go down the income scale. So, having less money causes more stress, and having more money supports less stress. This makes intuitive sense. If you have more money, you can deal with many different stressors. For instance, having money enables me to support my parents. It decreases my stress by removing the financial aspect of their illnesses.

There's no income limit to happiness: the higher the salary, the more options you have. But there is an income minimum: if you're struggling to pay for basic living expenses, you have fewer options, which makes happy choices more challenging. You'll need money to do things. Even if it doesn't require much money to do things, you'll need to have the time to do them.

YOUR TIME AND HAPPINESS

Having more money often comes with a higher degree of time ownership. Money can buy back time, allowing you to experience your day-to-day life differently.

But something interesting came up in my interviews: having more time didn't necessarily correlate with more happiness. You need to know what to do with your time to be happier. People who knew what they wanted had hobbies and their social lives were happier. They knew how to spend their time focusing on wellness activities.

In contrast, people who didn't know what they wanted were unhappy. They said having all the time in the world stressed them out. One person shared that he looks for busy work because too much time makes his mind run rampant. Another said he uses the time to make more money, but when he's lying in bed at night, he can't shake the feeling that something is missing.

If you want to be happier, use your time to pursue your interests, learn something new, work on a craft, enjoy a hobby, hang with friends, travel, and volunteer.

A study by Cassie Mogilner and Michael Norton suggests that shifting "attention toward time can lead people to be happier with the products they consume and in their lives more generally."[4] People who focused on time were more "motivated to socialize more and to work less," which corresponds with happiness.

The unfortunate reality: many people continue to exchange their time for money *for* stuff.

YOUR STUFF AND HAPPINESS

Some people "feel" happy because they can spend money. It leads to buying more and more stuff to get the dopamine hit. There will never be enough stuff to make you feel satisfied. And you'll realize there's never enough money to make you feel fulfilled.

Our human ability to adapt has been helpful in our species' survival. However, it's working against us in the modern society we've created.

We're trying to buy our way to happiness with stuff, but we adapt. Hedonic adaptation is the observed tendency of humans to quickly return to a relatively stable level of happiness despite major positive or negative events.[5]

It's why it's hard to buy happiness with stuff. It's never enough. The happy people with money I interviewed shared they were less focused on materialism and consumption.

A study published in the *Journal of Applied Research in Quality of Life* found life satisfaction is negatively impacted when people focus on materialism as a sign of a happy life. The researchers of "The Dual Model of Materialism" study shared that materialism in itself wasn't bad, but how we view it affects our life satisfaction. "Happy materialism" is when we see material consumption as a sign of happiness that leads to dissatisfaction. Since you don't have a high income or a luxury car, you can't be happy. It "lead[s] a person to not find satisfaction from other important areas of life,"[6] such as work, family, social life, and physical health. And as you'll learn, these are related to the wellness dimensions.

My nonscientific findings have led me to believe that focusing on wellness supports happiness. There's a connection between happiness and well-being: money is a connector.

CHAPTER 2

Money Isn't Everything

Before the pandemic, my mom and I planned to travel to the Philippines to visit my Lola (grandmother). We hadn't seen her for a few years. With my mom's medical issues, she would need me to come along, and I was more than happy to do so. It takes over 20 hours to fly from New Jersey to Manila. It's a long trip that takes a toll on the body.

We planned to fly in October 2019 but decided to wait for a "cheaper" flight outside the holiday season. I found the "best" airfare for a flight in April 2020. We could see my Lola and celebrate her 94th birthday.

Then the pandemic came. Everything stopped. Our flights were canceled. We waited in anticipation.

My mom and I never got to fly to the Philippines to see my grandmother. She died on my birthday in July 2020. I share this to say that not everything should be filtered through money. I would gladly pay the extra $500 per ticket to hug my Lola one last time. This is an example of not staying true to my core values (family) and not using my vision to guide me.

That experience affected me. I had the financial resources but chose not to use them to empower myself. Instead, I made a financial calculation, not a human connection. So when I hear money experts berate people for choosing joy over financial goals, I want to hug these experts and tell them that it's okay to use money to buy a little bit of happiness.

Money can be a filter but should not be the only deciding factor. There's more to a happy life than dollars and cents.

I understand money is the root of stress for many people. It was mine for many years. It took time to unpack and address the underlying causes. Doing the work proved to be vital: it prepared me to meet the financial stresses unleashed by the pandemic.

FINANCIALLY WELL AND HEALTHY

During the pandemic quarantine, my well-being was tested to its limits. Normally, when I am stressed, I will change my environment or hang out with friends. But we were in a global emergency, and I was alone and stuck in one place. The isolation tested my mental and emotional health. And in the early days of quarantine, I was failing miserably. I could not calm my fears and anxiety about the uncertainty of my physical health.

One evening, I was angrily tweeting in a social sea of angry tweeters. So many of us were afraid and fearful. I was about to send the best comeback tweet until I caught myself. My mindfulness practice alerted me to my downward spiral. I put the phone down, shut it off, and hid underneath my blanket. I woke up 12 hours later.

My body ached. I had a slight headache. I drank water to hydrate my brain. The sun was bright. I went out to the backyard and let its rays shower me. I felt the cool morning breeze touch my skin. I decided to do some light stretching. Something had changed.

I felt better. My body simply wanted to rest, but the fear that glued me to the news made me a nervous wreck who couldn't sleep. But I finally slept. I made a choice that morning to control what I could. I would focus on my mental, emotional, and physical health.

There was something unique about my situation.

When the world was uncertain about the economy, and people feared their financial livelihood, I was in a good place with money. My decision to break away from debt, focus on income streams, and save and invest prepared me financially to meet the global health uncertainty.

Even though my speaking gigs—my primary source of income—were halted for the unforeseen future, my finances gave me security and choices. I used my financial health to counterbalance other aspects of my well-being. I wanted to feel in control of something. So, I posted on Facebook, offering to pay for grocery deliveries to needy families.

Since I was isolated at home, I began a deeper yoga practice, pushing the limits of what I thought my body could do. By chance, I scrolled to an Instagram image of a yogi, Jonah Kest, offering an online yoga teacher program. I've always wanted to go through certification but never really "had the time." The cost was about $2,000: I didn't hesitate to make the decision. I *finally* had the time and the financial resources.

The yoga teacher training pushed my limits. It also served to support other aspects of my wellness. The yogic philosophy connected me to something greater (spiritual), and my cohorts of aspiring teachers gave me an online family (social). All of this was done in the comfort of my home (environmental), which served as my protected space.

And I wasn't alone in this experience.

I saw phroogal.com traffic grow 1,000% with the top articles on different ends of the spectrum, from investing and wealth creation to budgeting and making money at home. Financially healthy people were able to deal with the quarantine better than others. And people with specific careers could work from home and continue earning income. People with money were able to capitalize on the opportunities. It created new stock market investors and led to the frenzy of speculative bets in crypto and NFTs. And as communities were locked down, many with financial means bought homes to escape.

But many others had a different experience.

I've spoken to people who felt the intense pressure of financial obligations more than the threat to their physical health. They were suffering, unable to earn money to pay for basic necessities. The mental and emotional toll of being unable to work, socialize, or leave their apartments would affect their physical health. "I couldn't move," wrote a reader. "I was physically exhausted just thinking about how to put food on the table or pay for utilities."

According to a 2019 Capital One CreditWise survey, 73% of Americans surveyed consider finances as the biggest (#1) stress in their life, surpassing stress related to politics, family, and work.[1] Financial stress began way before the pandemic.

FINANCIALLY STRETCHED AND STRESSED

Financial stress is experienced mentally, expressed emotionally, and appears physically. It can affect your work, home, relationships, and sense of self. But we do experience financial stress differently. I've met people who are "barely getting by" living stressful lives. I've also met financially independent people stressed about money. Both examples highlight financial anxiety—a debilitating fear associated with money. It can be triggered by any situation, not just the lack of money.

Stress is a part of life. We have little daily stresses and, at times, big stresses that overwhelm us. Stress is a normal human reaction that happens to all of us.

"We're designed to experience stress to alert us of our environment," said my brother, John Vitug, a PhD candidate in applied behavior analysis.

"We think of stress as a bad thing," he adds, "but they are physical and mental responses to our environment. They are alerting us, but they can overwhelm us too."

When I've asked others about their stress, many describe it as something they feel internally. Rarely do people make the connection that it's a response to something external. Stress is the "fight or flight" response to a situation or environment.

"It raises stress hormones—cortisol and adrenaline," said John. "It causes mental and physical tension to get us in a state of readiness. Stress in small amounts isn't a problem," he said.

Stress is useful in specific situations. But, frequent stress is troublesome. During the days of chronic stress, I coped with unhealthy behaviors. I was overeating to feel satisfied and had way too many alcoholic drinks to loosen me up. I was spending money and using credit to feel in control: it only made financial issues a consistent stressor.

"Persistent stress can wreak havoc in your mind and body. The elevated stress hormones cause memory issues and mood changes, and increase blood pressure and heart rates," John said.

"It's the repeated stresses that can lead to mental health issues," he added.

When we don't address the situation or change the environmental causes of stress, our emotions and physical responses could alter our brain functioning.

Stress can lead to risky behaviors, resulting in poor health and creating financial challenges. For instance, continuing to spend way above your means makes it impossible to cover emergency expenses. It creates financial stress. Not addressing the spending habit often leads to experiencing financial stress repeatedly. It can result in financial anxiety: the mental health issue can make it challenging to change the actual behavior that perpetuates financial stress.

When you're financially well, you can respond effectively to financial challenges. You might not have the money now, but you're not overwhelmed with the situation either.

YOUR FINANCIAL HEALTH MATTERS

If you have financial issues, other parts of your life may be thrown off balance. If we can improve your financial health, we can also positively affect other areas of your life.

My friend Dr. Barbara O'Neill, a Distinguished Professor Emeritus at Rutgers University, was involved in a study called "Conceptualizing Health and Financial Wellness." The authors discovered that we can make "positive behavior changes to improve both health and personal finances simultaneously."[2]

Financial health is customizable to fit your personality, priorities, and goals. Think of physical health where a one-size-fits-all plan can't serve everyone. There needs to be room for adjustments and variations to achieve the goal—to be healthier.

The Consumer Financial Protection Bureau (CFPB) defines *financial health* as "how much your financial situation and money choices provide you with security and freedom of choice." The CFPB narrowed financial health down to four elements.[3]

1. Feeling in control
2. Capacity to absorb financial shock
3. On track to meet goals
4. Flexibility to make choices

As you can see, the elements support happiness studies. It boils down to our financial health, giving us more options and control over our time.

So, yes, you want to be financially healthy. I want you to say it: *I will be financially healthy.* Now, repeat it: *I will be financially healthy.* Don't be embarrassed to say it louder: *I will be financially healthy.*

In doing a simple intention exercise, I want you to understand you've just claimed financial wellness for yourself. That's an essential move. If you don't believe you can become financially healthy, then no books, tools, or programs can help. It starts with your mindset.

Take a moment and acknowledge the thoughts and feelings that are running through your mind. Notice your breath and feel the sensations in your body.

What are you thinking? How do you feel?

Let's turn a life with financial dis-*ease* into a life with more *ease*.

STRESS COPING TECHNIQUES

Use the following stress coping techniques.

Breathwork

Your breath changes when you're stressed. You'll notice fast and shallow breaths during stressful moments. The American Psychological Association wrote, "Stress and strong emotions can present with respiratory symptoms, such as shortness of breath and rapid breathing, as the airway between the nose and the lungs constricts."[4]

Focus on your breathing. Take intentional deep inhales and slow exhales. Use a four-second inhale and four-second exhale approach. Notice your breath.

Meditation

Meditation is not suppressing thoughts. It's an opportunity to let your mind rest in the present moment. New studies show meditation's positive impact on the brain and body.

A few minutes to interrupt a busy day can be enough to change your mood. Meditation is a mindfulness tool. Take a comfortable seated position or lie down. Close your eyes and focus on your breath. Follow the inhales and exhales. You're not manipulating the breath, just noticing.

Movements

Get up and move. Change your emotion and get into motion.

Start simple. Get up from where you're feeling stressed. Off the bed, couch, or desk. Get on your feet and give yourself a nice big stretch. Move your arms and start walking. Maybe you can walk out the door and stroll around the neighborhood.

Create

We're all creative in some way. The mindful shifting of attention from doing to creating can improve your well-being.

Stress can inspire your art. Let it flow into writing, painting, graphic design, crocheting, furniture building, and whatever else comes to mind when you think of creative works.

Connect with Friends

Engage with your friends, not discuss your situation. Simply being around others can be a good distraction from your thoughts.

Say "No"

Give yourself time and energy to deal with the situation causing your stress. Set boundaries and say "yes" to activities that help you relieve stress and resolve underlying issues.

CHAPTER **3**

But Money Impacts Most Things

'™ve wondered about happiness and other aspects of my life. Could I be happy and unhappy at the same time? Why am I excelling in one part of my life and free-falling in another? It seemed there were parts of me that were vying for attention. But I couldn't make the connection.

"You have to come," said Jessica. "It's going to be so much fun."

My trip to the Amalfi Coast was on a whim. *Could I afford it?* I wondered. Leaving for Italy wouldn't solve my legal problems or help with my health issues. It might add to the already tightening grip of finances around my neck. With each day, I was finding it harder to catch my breath. But maybe changing my environment was what I needed.

"I'm going. I'm booked," I texted her.

"We're going to Positano!" she said excitedly over the phone.

It was the first time I'd felt happy in a long time.

On my flight across the Atlantic, I read a book Jessica gave me, *What I Know for Sure*, by Oprah Winfrey.

Oprah wrote in one passage:

> None of us is built to run nonstop. That's why, when you don't give yourself the time and care you need, your body rebels in the form of sickness and exhaustion.[1]

I was exhausted. I was sick. I was also running nonstop. And my body had begun showing the wear and tear of the constant grind. It was time to step away. Fortunately, I had the credit card rewards and Airbnb credit that made the trip financially possible.

The spontaneous decision allowed me to take a pause. It gave me time to reflect. Being in a new environment and having different conversations also shifted my perspective.

On the third day of the trip, I woke up early to see the sunrise. The guest gathering area, a former family living room, had a breakfast spread of crackers, cheese, fruits, and yogurt. Everything looked Instagrammable.

"I lived in Brooklyn for a time," my host shared.

As I poured coffee into a cup, he continued, "It was a good time, but I miss life in Italy. We enjoy life. Things are slower."

"Slower can be good," I replied.

"Enjoy life. Eat. Drink. Meet people. Enjoy it," he said enthusiastically.

"It's why I'm here," I said, smiling back.

I headed for a table and chair on the balcony. The rising sun's light created a dazzling array of pink and orange hues that defined the lines of the mountainous coastline. I sat there enjoying the view and slowly sipped my coffee.

How did I get here? I whispered to myself. "I can't believe I am in Italy," I said loudly.

Just three days ago, I was experiencing a high level of anxiety. And yet, there I was, in no rush to be anywhere feeling gratitude. It was at that moment I made the wellness connection.

THE WELLNESS WHEEL

A *New York Times* article explained that the word *wellness* emerged in 1650 as the opposite of illness.[2] It was a healthy state of living achieved "without simply avoiding sickness" and as an actively pursued goal.

I relate to Iyanla Vanzant's definition of *health*. In a video, she shared:

> True health is a state of being that allows you to live productively, as you pursue the desires of your heart. Health means your mind is sound and clear; your body is nourished, nurtured, and flexible. Your heart is sound physically, emotionally peaceful, and joy-filled; your spirit is grounded and aligned with something higher than you, sustaining and supporting you as you move through life.[3]

Wellness isn't the absence of illness. It is a conscious and evolving process of making mindful decisions to live a more balanced and meaningful life. Health is how you're doing. Wellness is what you're doing.

Wellness is multidimensional and holistic, encompassing lifestyles, choices, and actions. The way you live, the joy and happiness you experience, is wellness. The way you respond to internal and external factors is wellness. It's more than physical and mental health. It encompasses so much more.

I was not the first to realize the connection between other areas of well-being. The concept was called the wellness wheel. It was a model based on the principle that people could live healthier and better lives if they understood the interrelatedness of various areas of their life. Dr. Bill Hettler, a co-founder of the National Wellness Institute, is credited for introducing the concept in 1976, showing six dimensions of wellness.

I dug deeper into research: Dr. Peggy Swarbrick, a research professor at Rutgers University, is recognized for the iteration of the six-dimension wheel to the eight dimensions concept. Dr. Swarbrick's version includes intellectual, emotional, physical, spiritual, social, occupational, environmental, and financial dimensions. The model showed that the dimensions are adjacent and overlapping, signifying how each dimension can impact one another.

IT'S INTERCONNECTED

We are multifaceted beings, and that's probably why so many of us struggle with happiness. Often we're focused on one area and neglect the others. The approach taken by many, including myself, is why we get burnt out doing work we love. It's why we feel insecure with a sizeable nest egg. It's why we don't own a home but own a bunch of stuff. It's why *I* chose to save on a plane ticket: I focused solely on money, not family.

There is a connection and a relationship among the wellness dimensions.

The further I researched, I discovered many variations of the wellness wheel. And whichever version is used, the idea behind any wellness wheel is simple: *there's an interconnectedness among dimensions.*

Knowing how one dimension is interconnected to another helps you make better decisions. Understanding how it affects multiple areas allows for a holistic approach. And learning your strengths can lead to improved well-being. We all have different strengths and areas we can strengthen and improve, so the approach to wellness becomes personalized. It enables you to choose to address a weaker area with your strengths.

Perhaps you're suffering from anxiety, and it's affecting your sleep (physical), causing an inability to concentrate (mental). Being physically and mentally exhausted, you cannot work (occupational). It's affecting your paycheck (financial), and now you're financially stressed, too.

You might address the financial stress by forcing yourself to work more hours. It'll only lead to more exhaustion and suffering. Using your knowledge of wellness dimensions, you recognize an opportunity to address emotional health—the ability to self-regulate and manage emotions—that can alleviate stress.

With the right coping techniques, you can sleep better and wake up mentally alert. It's given you back your mind and body to resolve the underlying issue creating the stress. Wellness is multidimensional, allowing you to *actively* work in one or more areas for overall well-being.

During a period of unhappiness, I leaned into my occupational and social wellness to counterbalance my ailing financial health. I reached out to friends and colleagues for support, enabling me to fix my money issues. It had a positive ripple effect on my mental, emotional, and physical health: I became happier.

That's when the connection became more evident. Research studies have pointed to different traits of happy people. You've read about them in a previous chapter. You've learned that happy people are continually learning (mental), emotionally intelligent (emotional), physically active (physical), do meaningful work (occupational), have a healthy social life (social), and give back to others (spiritual). And they aren't stressing about money (financial).

The research I've read and the nonscientific study I conducted led me to conclude that *wellness makes people happy long term*. It reduces the suffering and stress we might experience.

Many things cause stress: life changes, relationships, work, illness, parenthood, holidays, traffic, travel, politics, and money. And stressors change over time as your mind adapts to situations or responds to new behavior.

We experience stress differently.

What you find enjoyable might be stressful to others. I enjoy going on stage in front of thousands of people. I still get butterflies in my stomach, but I use it to deliver a great experience. A friend gets stage fright in front of people but is calm and collected when he jumps out of planes.

We experience stress dimensionally.

Trying to study for an exam can be mentally stressful. The ups and downs of a relationship are emotional stress. Working nonstop creates physical stress. The social pressure to "fit in" is stressful. Work demands, the cluttered space, the quest for meaning, and financial status—all affect our happiness. The stress we feel relates to mental, emotional, physical, social, spiritual, environmental, occupational, and financial dimensions.

We need to respond to stress within the dimension that's fostering it.

The daily commuting traffic stressed me out in one of my previous jobs. I'd get into the office in a bad mood. It made me unhappy at work. At first, I thought work was the problem and leaving the job was the answer. Instead, I decided to leave my house five minutes earlier to avoid the bottlenecks on the road. My response removed me from the situation causing the stress. It made me happier at work. That was an "aha" moment for me, when I realized that there's much I can't control (rush hour traffic), but there are things I can control (leaving earlier to avoid traffic).

When we deal with, overcome, and resolve stressors, we have a sense of control that fosters the feeling of happiness.

There is a happiness connection to wellness.

THE HAPPINESS CONNECTION

Financially healthy people are less stressed. When you're financially healthy, you have the resources—time and money—to work on improving other dimensions. And improving wellness leads to happiness.

I thought of the many ways money affected my life. When money was scarce, I experienced stress that affected my mental and physical health. I was too exhausted to think, work, and socialize. When money was abundant, I explored my curiosities, worked smarter, and rested well.

Money made my trip to the Amalfi Coast possible. The change in environment positively impacted my mood. The adventures with Jessica and her family gave me much-needed social interaction. Money paid for those excursions. And the healthcare I needed was possible because money made it affordable. All these things contributed to making the best decision to better my life. Money affects different parts of our lives in subtle yet profound ways.

When it comes to financial stress, your emotions tell you something about a money situation that doesn't feel right. You can address the situation properly after identifying what's causing your stress. Because there's *a solution to every financial situation.*

I've learned money isn't the end all and be all, but it makes things possible. And it's the "possible things" we want more of. The possibility to own a home, go on a dream trip, spend time with friends, do meaningful work, and so on. Because these *possibilities* make us feel happier.

And it so happens these "possibilities" correlate with *wellness things* like mental, emotional, physical, spiritual, environmental, social, financial, and occupational.

It all came together: money isn't everything, but it impacts most *things*. Money can buy happiness by supporting *wellness*.

Wellness Things	
Mental	Mental wellness is the intellectual and cognitive ability to process, learn, grow, and use information.
Emotional	Emotional wellness is understanding, perceiving, managing, and expressing your emotions and relating with others.
Physical	Physical wellness is having healthy behaviors and daily habits that support your physical body.
Spiritual	Spiritual wellness is the values and beliefs that provide a sense of meaning and purpose to your life.
Environmental	Environmental wellness is interaction with the physical spaces you inhabit, fostering inner peace, safety, health, and connection.
Social	Social wellness is a sense of belonging and the ability to engage with others in a meaningful way, genuinely.
Financial	Financial wellness is a feeling of security and satisfaction with your current and future money situation.
Occupational	Occupational wellness is your sense of satisfaction, enrichment, and meaningful contribution through work.

How can you buy happiness?

You'll learn it's about spending on the wellness things that improve the quality of your life.

CHAPTER 4

Money Can Buy Happiness

On one particular morning, I was feeling run down. I had work deadlines to meet, but I didn't want to do anything. I had an overwhelming feeling of anxiousness. And everything went into a downward spiral once I checked social media. I was bombarded with terrifying news. I looked at my bed and wanted to crawl back in, but I remembered the wellness dimensions.

What area could I use to counterbalance my current state of mental distress? I decided to change my environment. I fixed up my bed and took my dog for a walk. We spent the early morning watching the sunrise. The change of environment and the physical movement affected my mental attitude for the day. I got work done. And I felt happier.

My financial health allows me to work for myself. I get to pick my work and the people I work with. This reduces stress in my life. Some people say "money can't buy happiness." I know one thing for sure: money bought me happiness that morning. Money gave me the option of how, when, and where to start my day.

Money can buy happiness when it's used to improve wellness because those purchases give us choices, options, time, and freedom.

Can money buy happiness?

I asked a hundred people, and the results weighed heavily in the "yes" column. Interestingly enough, every single person followed their "yes" or "no" response with a "but, let me explain." And not surprisingly, they were all in agreement that money can pay for the necessities of life but doesn't answer the burning question of the "meaning of life."

Here's the truth: **money can buy happiness, but money *isn't* happiness.**

If money *is* happiness, then you know what needs to be done. You need to take a job that pays a lot of money and we actually know which jobs do. But there's a good chance that, even knowing which job pays the most money, you want something more. You want to be happy. I would have taken a job on Wall Street if all I wanted was money: I didn't. I was driven by something else. I'm sure I would have made a lot more money in a short period of time, but I have no regrets about my decision. Choosing a credit union over an investment firm is part of my story that's led to a happy life.

What choices have you made to choose happiness over money?

MONEY WEAVES ITSELF INTO EVERYTHING

Let's start with some basics. Money means different things to different people. I've heard people say money is power, money is evil, money is freedom, and money is security.

What is money to you?

Money is _____ (fill in the blank). I've used this exercise in my talks and wrote about it in *You Only Live Once*. It's an impactful question that allows you to uncover your relationship with money. But I'll go ahead and state the following:

- Money is a tool.
- Money is a resource.
- Money is a value.
- Money is an exchange.
- Money is energy.

It really is just a means of transfer. We use money as the middle-person. If everyone decided they didn't want money, it would become worthless. Or we'd just find a different form of exchange. Crypto, anyone?

Money solves money problems.

When I was mentally and emotionally struggling, I felt extremely unhappy, but money allowed me to make purchases. These purchases gave me an escape from the struggles. But, I eventually realized there would never be enough money to solve my life problems.

I recently watched Casey Neistat's Youtube video *Being Rich vs. Being Poor*,[1] in which he explained how money solves money problems but can't solve life problems. Casey said it'll probably take a lifetime to solve life problems. But one thing was clear to him: people who say money can't solve problems have never been broke.

Money problems	Life problems
▪ Housing	▪ Happiness
▪ Food	▪ Purpose
▪ Healthcare	▪ Fulfillment
▪ Childcare	▪ Meaning
▪ Clothing	▪ Love
▪ Transportation	▪ Inner Peace

I've been unhappy and broke. I've had money and been unhappy. If money can't buy happiness, being broke can't buy anything. Having money and being unhappy was a much better situation than being broke. It was less stressful. I was happier whenever I had money to pay for money problems. And if you're broke and got a flush of money, you'll be happy too.

If you have a problem, figure out whether it's a money or a life problem. It's a money problem if you can use money to solve it. Need a car? Affording a car is a money problem. You'll need to make more money if you don't have money. That's the solution to money problems.

A life problem can be a money problem if you can assign a financial budget to it. Do you feel lonely? Can you assign a financial budget to the problem? If not, it's a life problem. But, if loneliness is due to geographical distance from friends, you can throw money at it (buy an airline ticket) to solve the problem.

Don't try to solve life problems with money.

I had a reader share that he was unhappy at work and bought a new car to feel in control. He realized too late that he had just trapped himself in a toxic job. Another was looking for a relationship and bought designer clothes on credit. She said, "I ended up marrying debt." The issue with throwing money at life problems is how often it misses the target.

You can use money to fix life issues.

For instance, save enough money to cover a few months of expenses if you want to leave a bad job. Buy happiness by quitting the job to look for a new career. Do you want to attract a good partner? Surround yourself with new people by buying classes to explore an interest. It might not lead to a spouse, but at the very least, you've learned a new skill.

I'm not here to tell you how to spend your money. However, I want to challenge your thinking about how you spend it. Because there are better ways to spend.

What I hope money will buy.

Ninety-nine percent of the world has a price tag. We place a monetary cost on everything, including humanitarian aid. We say things like we can't afford to help others in need. It's too expensive to offer childcare or healthcare or a college education. Things we know people need (and may even want for ourselves) and say there simply isn't enough money to afford it. Money would solve those problems. And if we could solve those money problems, we could collectively try to answer humanity's life problems.

Unfortunately, the human race isn't there yet. But there's hope for you—an opportunity to be the oddity—to achieve financial freedom and find answers to your life problems.

HOW MONEY BUYS HAPPINESS

Money can buy happiness because it gives us the means to solve money-related problems. We are happier when we can afford housing, food, healthcare, and clothing. And once the basics are covered, money frees our time and mental space to pursue a purposeful life.

Talking about passion and purpose is challenging when you're financially stressed. But the reality is such that you're probably still thinking about purpose as you dodge your landlord. That's because you are a multifaceted person composed of eight interconnected wellness dimensions.

Money can buy happiness but only up to a point.

Money can pay for dates but can't buy love. Money can buy you time, but not a purpose. Money can buy you a home, but not inner peace. People throw money at life problems and wonder why they aren't being fixed. If money was indeed the only answer, then we should stop chasing dreams, marrying for love, having kids, and whatever it is that gives meaning to life.

There's a reason wealthy people say "money isn't important." It's because they realize their life issues aren't solved by simply having more money. Gaining a sense of fulfillment and contentment goes far beyond money's capabilities. The life goals you want money can't directly buy.

- Money can't buy **meaning** (*occupational*).
- Money can't buy **wisdom** (*mental*).
- Money can't buy **inner peace** (*emotional*).
- Money can't buy **health** (*physical*).
- Money can't buy **memories** (*social*).
- Money can't buy **security** (*environmental*).
- Money can't buy **satisfaction** (*financial*).
- Money can't buy **purpose** (*spiritual*).

Money may not be able to buy these life goals, but being financially healthy can help you work towards them. That's why you must prioritize financial health to remove the financial barriers. And here's an important thing about life goals: you don't need to reach specific financial milestones to work on them either.

Spend on the right things.

Buying the new Rolex might make you happy for a time, but buying a workshop that teaches you how to paint will make you happier long term. I chose the painting workshop.

I bought my parents a mini-van. They were thankful and happy when I handed them the car's title—free and clear of any loans. As months passed, my parents commented on maintenance and insurance expenses. I realized the feeling of happiness had waned. So, I took them on a cross-country road trip in that mini-van. They still talk about their experiences on the road. The car is utilitarian, but the road trip was experiential.

Happiness is an emotional response to a situation or environment. For example, if you got a new job, got engaged, had a baby, graduated college, or got divorced, your situation has changed positively, resulting in happiness.

Money changes your situation through purchases. How do you feel after buying a new car, buying limited-edition sneakers, or upgrading your smartphone? You're happy because you've changed something in your life through these purchases. But the happy feeling from buying stuff is fleeting.

It led happiness researchers in one study to write: "The relationship between money and happiness is surprisingly weak, which may stem in part from the way people spend it."[2]

If you want the happy feeling to last longer, you want to make better purchases that contribute to life satisfaction and well-being.

Money buys your way out of everyday stresses.

A 2021 study found that money can improve lives because money solves little nuisances. The research paper proposed, "While money may not necessarily buy happiness, it reduces the intensity of stressors experienced in daily life—and thereby increase life satisfaction."[3] If you get a flat tire, you have money to fix it. If your furnace breaks, you have money to replace it. Money solves little nuisances, but money can also solve many more stressors.

Money buys your way out of life challenges.

You can buy happiness when you're intentionally spending to change a situation or your environment. Money allows you to own your time, quit the job, leave a loveless marriage, learn a new skill, pay for conveniences, afford fitness trainers, gain new experiences, live in a nicer home, and pursue a deeper meaning.

Money buys your way into purpose.

Jo Koy is a Filipino-American standup comedian. His rise to fame included multiple Netflix and Comedy Central specials. He holds the record as the only single artist to sell the most tickets in a Honolulu concert hall.

Most people don't know how Jo Koy risked his financial health to pursue happiness. Before the rise, his pitch to studios for a comedy special was rejected seven times. His growth mindset would not allow him to give up. Jo Koy used all of his money to create a comedy special to show the studios why he deserved space at the table. He smashed the performance, and Netflix bought his special. That led to multiple deals and the movie *Easter Sunday*.

The Happy Money lesson: Jo Koy bought happiness through better work instead of buying stuff to cope with the rejections. He went from a retail job to selling out arenas worldwide, becoming the most recognizable comedian of our time.

During an interview on KTLA 5, Jo Koy shared that as the crowd laughed at his punchlines, he was thinking how broke he was. He cried while sharing the story, and I could see the psychological effect of choosing happiness.

I met Jo Koy in 2015 at the White House before his first Netflix special. Even back then, he was always giving back, believing that if you can help others, do it. Jo Koy's success is shared by the Fil-Am community he proudly represents on stage. And he's known for his charitable and helping nature, inspiring others to believe in their dreams.

Jo Koy bought happiness by changing the trajectory of his career (occupational). I made a similar change and bought a life experience: backpacking around the world (emotional). My yearlong journey exposed me to new ideas and concepts. It transformed me. It's why this book is in your hands.

Money plays a role in our lives, but so many use it to buy stuff, believing it's happiness. Money is a tool to create a happy life. Use the money to buy these things:

- Money can buy you better work (*occupational*).
- Money can buy you education (*mental*).
- Money can buy you boundaries (*emotional*).
- Money can buy you healthcare (*physical*).
- Money can buy you experiences (*social*).
- Money can buy you comforts (*environmental*).
- Money can buy you time (*spiritual*).
- Money can buy you assets (*financial*).

Remember this: . . . in pursuit of _____ (fill in the blank). And focus on buying *things* that support your wellness: buy back your time for better work. Buy home cleaning services so you can rest. Buy dinner for a friend and have a fun conversation. Buy your way out of the unsafe neighborhood. Buy a trip to Bali to find yourself. You get the idea. There are certain activities that money can buy that support happiness.

In the *How of Happiness*, author Sonja Lyubomirsky, PhD, introduces the happiness pie chart, showing that happiness is part genetics (50%), part environment (10%), and part activity (40%). There is nothing we can do about genetics, and we have little impact on external situations, but the study posits that 40% of happiness is for us to make through intentional behaviors to improve well-being.[4] Imagine having the ability to be 40% happier.

How would you change your spending behaviors?

A key to happiness is changing behaviors that don't suit you. Using what you're learning in this book, you can make an intentional change by spending mindfully.

Two previous Happy Money books use two different approaches—science and art—that teach you how to spend for happiness.

Elizabeth Dunn and Michael Norton, co-authors of *Happy Money* (2014), shared five ways to spend money for happiness. They are: buy experiences (emotional and social), make it a treat (emotional), buy time (occupational), pay now and consume later (mental), and invest in others (social and spiritual).

Another *Happy Money* (2019) book by Ken Honda shared the Japanese philosophy, artistry, and flow of money. It centered on the interconnectedness between money and emotions. His ideas include: dealing with past traumas (emotional), shifting how you think (mental), better work relationships (occupational), donating money (spiritual), and finding your tribe (social).

You can see how their spending recommendations fit within the wellness dimensions. So if you've been wondering how to define a nebulous emotion like happiness, use the wellness dimensions. Spend to affect each dimension through a mindful approach using money as a tool, a resource, a value, an exchange, and as energy to achieve your goals. You'll learn how in Book II.

What will you buy to change your situation for happiness and wellness?

BOOK II

Happy Life

Very little is needed to make a happy life; it is all within yourself.

—Marcus Aurelius

've switched things up. I'm making you start with the end in mind—
your happy life. You'll get all the financial strategies and tips in Book
III—your happy money.

My journey into financial wellness started with a realization that
there is more to life than chasing money, but money is necessary to
pursue dreams happily. In my short time in this world, I have accom-
plished many things. I excelled in professional pursuits that supported
my financial health. But my relentless drive for professional success
led to mental, emotional, and physical exhaustion.

I believed doing more of the work I enjoyed would help my issues.
It did the opposite. Those issues began affecting how I viewed working. My work was no longer a sense of pride but a hindrance to my
happiness.

With a better understanding of wellness dimensions, I learned
to use my financial health (my strengths) to counterbalance and
strengthen other areas. I stopped mindlessly spending, and I better
aligned my money with life goals. I've accepted that there's not much
I can control in this world. But I *can* control how I earn, manage, and
spend money. Doing so improved my mental health. And that led to

managing my time better to ensure I give myself adequate rest, nutri-tion, and exercise—physical wellness.

My financial wellness gave me the confidence to stop relying on social media for validation. It had a positive impact on my emotional health. I didn't need to show how much I hustled to feel worthy of attention. I didn't need to brag about living *the* life; I was simply liv-ing *my* life.

I also stopped comparing myself to online entrepreneurs and influencers because my financial health gave me peace of mind. I used my financial resources to improve my living conditions and cultivate a safe and rejuvenating space. And I began spending more quality time with friends strengthening my social well-being.

These choices have led to a happier life. I've grown my mantra: *you only live once, make it a happy life.*

HAPPY DIMENSIONS

Your happy life consists of eight wellness dimensions—mental, emo-tional, physical, spiritual, social, occupational, environmental, and financial. I refer to them as the **happy dimensions.**

Happy dimensions are interconnected and overlapping. Working on one dimension affects the others. Learning your dimensional strengths can help to counterbalance areas that need strengthening. You don't have to address all dimensions. You can be tactful with your approach.

Wellness makes the elusive idea of happiness more tangible.

Instead of hoping to feel happy, focus your time, effort, and money on a dimension that improves well-being. The result is more happiness.

Perhaps, you are struggling with a relationship and feeling stressed (emotional). It's affecting your ability to think clearly (mental). It's making you sluggish and exhausted (physical) and causing you to miss work (occupational). It's leading to smaller paychecks that are insuf-ficient to pay your bills (financial). You're now financially stressed, too. But you have supportive family and friends (social) who can help you with your troubled relationship. Use your strength to counterbalance your problems.

Without awareness of the dimensions, your problems lead you to make decisions that continue your struggles. For instance, you might choose to work more hours to pay bills, hurting your social interactions and reducing your time to work on the relationship. You haven't solved the underlying stressor.

Or maybe you excel at work (occupational) and are rewarded with higher pay (financial), but all the time spent working took you away from your family and friends (social) and left you with little time to rest or sleep (physical). Your moods have changed (mental and emotional). And as you lie in bed at night, you question your place in the world (spiritual). Counterbalance these problems by using your financial health to work fewer hours, spend time with friends, and give to a purposeful cause. This will lead to a change in mood and attitude, supporting your overall well-being.

It can seem overwhelming, but knowing how everything is all related, you can work on one area and affect other dimensions.

In Book II, Happy Life, you'll gain insights into each dimension and learn how the happy dimensions connect with one another. Understanding each of these dimensions can be a book of its own. Perhaps, one day they will be. But for now, the focus is to share how money buys happiness by impacting wellness.

In the following chapters, you'll learn how to improve each dimension from a financial perspective, giving you better routines and habits. Even if your financial health needs improving, you will gain knowledge to help you live better. And it will make your money journey in Book III all the more exciting.

As you progress through the happy dimensions, you'll understand the interconnectedness and how the framework can help you choose happiness. There is no hierarchy to these dimensions, but I have ordered the chapters intentionally.

Book II includes the following chapters.

Happy Dimensions	Happy Principles
Chapter 5: Happy Money (Financial)	Live financially free.
Chapter 6: Happy Work (Occupational)	Rewire; don't retire.
Chapter 7: Happy Mind (Mental)	Invest in yourself and learn continually.
Chapter 8: Happy Heart (Emotional)	Memories appreciate; stuff depreciates.
Chapter 9: Happy Body (Physical)	Be kind to your body; it's priceless.
Chapter 10: Happy Social (Social)	Connections are your lifeline.
Chapter 11: Happy Space (Environmental)	Free your space and yourself.
Chapter 12: Happy Spirit (Spiritual)	Serve a purpose, not a purchase.

You can now enter your first dimension.

Poetic
Introduction

Remember:

Someone will remember you, but...
No one will remember how much you made.
No one will remember the investments.
No one will remember the credit score.
No one will remember the debt you hid.
Someone will remember how you made them feel.
They will remember the time invested.
They will remember laughing to the core.
They will remember the good you did.
Someone will remember the life you lived.
What will you remember?

CHAPTER **5**

Happy Money

Living Financially Free

L iving financially free is the ultimate goal.

You're free to make life decisions that are not solely filtered through finance. You recognize financial goals but don't sacrifice life goals. You can live financially free when you're debt free, financially secure, in retirement, or financially independent. You don't have to wait until a financial milestone is reached, so start developing your mindset and behaviors.

Living financially free is about your thoughts, feelings, and habits allowing you to live with more joy and happiness.

Financial wellness is Happy Money. It's your ability to meet current and future financial needs. You have a good understanding of personal finance, can manage money, control credit, and invest for the future. You're financially healthy and living well today while building a better tomorrow.

"I'm really happy," said Michelle, answering my question about being financially free. "I am enjoying the life we've created. I love what I do and don't see myself not doing it."

Michelle Schroeder-Gardner, 33, is a mom, business owner, blogger, and founder of makingsenseofcents.com. She reached financial freedom over five years ago. During those years, Michelle lived in an RV traveling across the United States and spent four and half years sailing the Caribbean with her husband (Happy Space). She did all this while running her six-figure business (Happy Work).

I admire her business savviness and commitment to living well (Happy Heart). I followed her travels from the hikes up sun-scorched mountains to backcountry driving to their first sail in the Bahamas (Happy Body). She shared the adventures in her candid blog posts about income reports and her desire to work fewer hours (Happy Mind).

"There was a time when I worked 100 hours a week," she said. "It helped get the blog to where it is."

Although Michelle's initial motivation to blog was an outlet to share, it quickly grew and began earning income. After paying off over $40,000 of student loans, she realized the side hustle could become a full-time opportunity. She quit her $45,000 job to run a business that makes, on average, $800,000 per year in the last five years (Happy Money).

"Will you retire early?" I asked.

"I really love my work," she said, smiling. "I don't work many hours, and it's fun."

Michelle considers herself financially independent. But she won't stop working anytime soon as she finds purpose in her work (Happy Spirit). Michelle works about 10 hours per week, earning passive income that allows her freedom to be with her family (Happy Social).

"What has achieving financial independence meant?" I asked.

"I have more control over my time and work," she replied.

Michelle is an exception.

There are examples of financially independent people who don't feel that sense of control. I've met many in my travels through the years. And in private conversations, they'll share their mental struggles. It was surprising initially to learn how they were still experiencing anxiety and stress about money. I noticed a common habit among the stressed and financially independent group. They continue to filter every life decision through money.

"There doesn't seem to be enough," said one blogger who retired at 38 years old.

That seems to be a running theme among people who believe reaching financial independence would solve all their problems.

"We got back the time from our jobs, but now it's like what do we do," he said. "It's easy to default back to making money because that's what we've been doing."

I will admit it's probably this trait of filtering decisions through money that enabled them to reach financial independence. *But, at what cost?* I've wondered.

"We're trying not to spend over our budget and always looking for ways to make money. We even moved away from family to have a lower cost of living, and it's made me miserable," he shared.

A study by a Princeton University psychologist "found a powerful link between concerns over financial security and satisfaction with one's life."[1] The study found that women who concentrated their thinking on financial matters were much less happy. And those who "didn't fixate on finances" reported being the happiest. Surprisingly, the women in the study group "had plenty of money," suggesting that "financial security, more than money alone, may be key to happiness."

In my artful nonscientific study, I've met financially independent people who only filter life decisions through finances. It doesn't make them feel any more secure. They're constantly thinking about "having enough" money. It creates feelings of insecurity that keep them from living financially free.

Michelle, however, feels secure in her finances. It's given her the freedom to make bold choices about how to live. She's not held back by the fear some have "that it's not enough." Michelle and her husband don't rely on investments to pay for basic living expenses. Their independence comes from passive income generated from the blog. Michelle continues to work because she enjoys it. That choice and control over her time support the unique lifestyle they've built.

I've shared Michelle's story to highlight our journeys and lifestyle differences. However, we both are living financially free. We get to spend our time as we wish. We aren't fixating on financial numbers, which allows us to make life choices that contribute to our happiness.

Making money is not the priority; living life is. And interestingly enough, the moment you make that mindset shift, money has a tendency to follow and flow into your life.

HOW TO LIVE FINANCIALLY FREE

You don't have to wait until you reach financial freedom. It is less about financial numbers and more about ownership of your time and feeling financially secure. It's when you can be and live however you want without the trappings of finances. You're living the life you choose.

Living like this requires shifting your thinking, feeling, and doing, which can occur at any moment in your life journey. Living financially free means you save purposefully, earn effortlessly, spend mindfully, invest intentionally, give graciously, and live purposefully. Your approach to time and money will change to support happiness.

Evolve Your Beliefs

Challenge your beliefs about what it means to live well. Your time is the most valuable resource you're born with. But we are taught to exchange that time for money. We're left to believe money will solve life problems: it does not. Money will solve many of your problems but it will not buy the inner peace and security you desire. No amount of money will make you feel secure if you don't cultivate a healthier mindset.

Understanding my thoughts and feelings enabled me to improve my relationship with time and money. It led to a shift into positive thinking. I feel less constrained, allowing me to enjoy the fruits of my labor.

"Has it been an easy journey?" I asked.

"It has been challenging, but I believe in being positive," Michelle replied.

"Can you explain what it is about positivity that's helped you get to where you are?"

"It's really a mindset and being positive. There's a lot that goes on, and it's tough. I stay away from negativity and news," she added. "I rather focus on being positive."

The research shows that a growth mindset and positivity support happiness and well-being. You'd think being happy would give you a positive mindset, but having a positive mindset leads to happiness.[2]

You might be familiar with the "glass half full or half empty" exercise. People are asked how they see a glass on the table. If you respond that it's half full, you're an optimist. If you respond that it's half empty, you're a pessimist. There's no conclusive evidence that either is correct. But a study has found that "optimism may significantly influence mental and physical well-being."[3]

What has supported my optimistic view has been the positive changes I've made in how I use my time and money.

Save Purposefully

Saving money is securing inner peace. When saving, you have an optimistic view of life, believing you will be around to enjoy the money you saved. And when you give your savings purpose, you're honoring your time.

You can afford and enjoy everything you want, but you can't do it all at once. Savings goals allow you to prioritize and direct your money purposefully. Having savings helps you experience less stress.

- **Savings for income disruptions.** Have money available to cover unexpected expenses or periods of underemployment or medical emergencies.
- **Savings to limit credit use.** Less reliance on credit to cover purchases leads to lower debt obligations and to less financial stress in the future.
- **Savings for wealth creation.** Saving purposefully leads to growing your money (making money with money).
- **Savings to buy things too.** Enjoy purchasing guilt-free.

How are you saving your time?

Earn Effortlessly

Don't get in the way of money.

You want to earn as much as possible from your primary job. Then give your earnings a job too—have it work for you. Stop exchanging more of your time for a paycheck. You can earn effortlessly by making money with money.

There are many ways to increase income, from earning more at your job to side hustling for extra cash. The financially free choose to focus on passive income streams, which require less effort and time in the long run. There are three income categories: active, passive, and portfolio. Portfolio income can be considered a subset of passive income.

When you stop exchanging your time for a paycheck, you regain hours to focus on your health and interests. *What projects could you work on? What places could you explore?*

Michelle created a life based on passive income. She recommends that more people focus on income streams that can turn into passive sources. "Some passive sources may require a lot of time early on," she says, "but as it grows, it may require less and continue to make money."

How are you making time?

Passive income	Portfolio income
▪ Rental property	▪ Interest from savings accounts, certificates, etc.
▪ Royalties from book	
▪ Online shop	▪ Interest paid from lending
▪ Blogging	▪ Dividends
▪ Content creator	▪ Capital gains
▪ Business profits	

Spend Mindfully

Spend on what matters most to you. Otherwise, you're wasting your time. Don't exchange your time for nonvalue-added stuff.

Cultivate the skill to get what you need and want. It's not about choosing the cheapest option or depriving yourself of the best things in life. You can spend on nice things. I purchase experiences more than stuff. But when I do buy stuff, I focus on quality and usability, not merely price and quantity. I want the best product I can get for the lowest price. Although I am willing to pay a premium if it solves a problem, saves time, or is for convenience.

Michelle and her husband bought a sailboat. Their finances have allowed them to do many things and buy anything, but they spend mindfully on what they value. After owning an RV and a sailboat, they bought a home in the mountains for their next adventure: raising their daughter.

Your spending habits begin early and are influenced by how family and friends handle their own finances. Basically, your parents' money skills and friends' spending habits influence your spending. When you include the influences of advertising and social media, you can see that your spending decisions are not always your own. When you are not mindful, you can buy things that take you away from important things. Here's the difference between mindfully and habitually spending.

- *Mindfully spending* is when you're conscious of how you're spending and where you're spending money. You're aware of your choices and notice the signs of retail therapy, bargain shopping, and the lure of one-day sales.
- *Habitual spending* is automatic and often without thought. You're spending because you've been programmed to do so. And often, you don't question these purchases because they are ingrained in your everyday life.

How are you spending your time?

Invest Intentionally

Secure your future in an unpredictable world. Investing your money allows it to grow to ensure that your future time is about enjoyment, not employment.

Investing must remain a top priority. There are different forms of investing, such as rental properties, business ventures, and the stock market. You can diversify your investment strategy depending on your risk tolerance and interests.

Michelle and her husband continue to invest in their future. "We'll retire one day," she says, "it's important to invest because you really never know what will happen."

I invest for retirement and independence. I know all too well that my mind or body won't be up to snuff one day. I'm securing my future well-being by investing. I also keep my investments simple. I want less complexity in my life.

However you choose to invest, be intentional about how it will affect your happiness and well-being. If dealing with tenants stresses you out, then rental properties may not be ideal. And if the idea of losing money because of someone else's bad decisions will keep you up at night, then pass on the business opportunity. Whether you buy rental properties or more stocks, the goal is to grow your income-producing assets for greater peace of mind.

How are you investing your time?

Give Graciously

Charity is an essential part of well-being. You can help others financially or by offering your skills and time.

What is the purpose of all the money you've made if you can't do any good in the world? You don't have to wait to reach a financial milestone to give. Chances are good that you have something to give.

Giving to charities or other causes improves our mood. A study at Utah State University demonstrated that "using brain-scanning technology show[s] increased activation in the reward area of the brain, when giving to charities." Essentially, "giving to charity makes us happier; especially when we freely choose to give."[4] And as you've learned in Book I, money gives you choices. You can choose to give to feel happy.

When I began my financial wellness road trips, people all across the country graciously gave their time to support my cause. It showed how people are inherently charitable—from my friend Tiffany "The

Budgetnista" Aliche, who has given her attention to my causes, to Michelle, who took time away from her family to share her story for this book.

People's gracious giving has informed how I approach business and life. I give my time. I offer my skills. And I donate to causes. I've mentored college students, served as a board member at nonprofits, raised money for causes, and supported entrepreneurs worldwide.

When thinking about living financially free, consider the freedom to support purpose-driven people and worthy causes that fill your spirit, not just your pocket.

How are you giving time?

Live Prosperously

Choose to see the world with abundance. Truly enjoy the time you have in this lifetime.

Living prosperously means seeing more opportunities than anyone can do in a lifetime. You're not hoarding resources. There is enough for everyone. You're living in a state of enoughness. And choosing what's right for you.

I've learned what it means to live prosperously. I no longer compare myself to others. I cheer for their success and support their causes. I won't sacrifice my well-being for profit either. I have gratitude for what is and for what is to come. Living purposefully, for me, is no longer chasing money but pursuing my dreams and allowing money to follow.

Michelle has felt the same way. She shared a story of being docked next to $100 million dollar yachts. She recalls saying to herself how grateful she was for her sailboat even though it was a fraction of the price of those yachts. "We had the same views," she shared, "I didn't need to compare myself. We're still enjoying the same thing everyone is enjoying."

"What contributed to that type of thinking?" I asked.

"I can control my time and choose what I do. That taught me I could control my thoughts and choose to see the world with positivity and gratitude," Michelle said.

Living financially free has given Michelle a new perspective. She's living prosperously with the life she's created, not passively being affected by what others have.

There are many things you can't control, but one thing you can control is how you choose to see the world. External factors can influence your perspective, but mindful practices inform your response.

THE DIMENSIONS OF MONEY

You buy happiness in Happy Money by regaining your time. This is done with awareness and prioritizing time as your most valuable resource. You're saving time, earning time, spending time, investing time, and giving time to have an entire lifetime of purpose.

Living financially free comes from having money that enables you to own your time. Full control over your time allows you to pursue whatever brings you joy and happiness. But, as you've read, it can also cause stress.

"If you don't know what you'll be doing with the time," says Dr. Barbara O'Neill, "it can affect your health and sense of well-being." My semi-retired friend, Dr. Barb, shared stories of retirees who regained their time but lost their sense of purpose after retirement. It led many onto an emotional rollercoaster affecting their mental health.

Do you know how you will spend your time?

If you think you'll figure that out once you've hit a financial milestone, you may be shocked to learn it's not so. Waiting until financial milestones are reached prevents you from experiencing life and discovering your interests.

Start with the end goal in mind. Shift your beliefs and evolve your practices. Often what we seek can be accessible to us now.

In the next chapters, you'll learn about the remaining seven dimensions and how money affects them. You'll also discover how each dimension affects your financial health.

Work and money: Your desire for fancy job titles and higher salaries can lead to overwork and burnout. But work is essential to wellness. Find the balance of work and leisure. Enjoy the benefits of contribution, teamwork, and meaningful work.

Mind and money: Mental health issues are rising, spurred by economic uncertainty and financial vulnerability. You can learn how to improve mental health through a growth mindset of curiosity, continuous learning, and gaining skills.

Heart and money: Emotional health is how you feel in situations and in environments. Learn to assess, perceive, and respond to feelings. Increase your emotional intelligence to manage and cope with uncomfortable feelings. And create more memories that uplift your mood.

Body and mind: Your health is wealth. Take care of your physical health: exercise, sleep, and eat healthily. Make time for your body. Hustling and grinding to reach financial goals lead to exhaustion and the need for medical intervention. Burnout leads to unproductivity affecting financial health.

Social and money: Social interactions are vital to well-being. Sacrificing connections for financial goals will make for a lonely life. Studies show happy people have active and healthy social relationships. Continue making friends and nurturing your existing relationships.

Space and money: The places you occupy must be inviting, safe, and secure to allow you the space to be yourself. Overspending on needless items clutters your home and increases stress levels. Enjoying the free outdoors enhances your mood and inspires you.

Spirit and money: The nagging feeling of something missing is the spiritual void, a lack of connection to something greater than yourself. It's your calling. Your purpose. Your legacy. Create, don't simply consume. Add to the human experience, give to others, and practice gratitude.

In Book III, you'll learn more about the specific money strategies and tactics to improve your financial health. You can skip ahead if you'd like. For now, let's get you to Happy Work.

YOUR HAPPY TO-DO LIST

- **Give yourself a mental break.** We all need a form of escapism to relax and rest. You can read, binge shows, or paint. And you can meditate, do breathwork, and go for a walk. Your brain needs rest so that it can make better financial decisions.

- **Check in with your emotions**. What you *feel* is happening isn't necessarily what *is* happening. We can learn to express our emotions and not be ruled by them, so that we're less susceptible to spending.

- **Don't sacrifice your physical health.** Take care of your body, so that you don't spend your money paying for medical bills. Be healthy enough to enjoy your wealth.

- **Spend time with friends.** Imagine having all that money and no one to enjoy it with. Value your social connections and memories gained from experiences.

CHAPTER 6

Happy Work

Rewire; Don't Retire

You're probably burnt out from work because of a misalignment, not from overworking. Most people who say they want to retire only want to take a break. Or find something else to do. The most interesting finding from my nonscientific study was how much work was important for someone's sense of self. It's important to rethink work.

Occupational wellness is Happy Work. It comes from your sense of satisfaction, enrichment, and meaningful contribution through productivity. Happy Work is when you're balancing work with leisure and doing exactly what you want to do that is both satisfying and financially rewarding. With that said, you don't sacrifice other parts of your life for professional achievements.

"I gave 300% for 20 years, and it meant nothing," Amanda shared.

Amanda Girardi, 43, is a small business owner making the most delicious treats and baked goods. She is an extremely talented cook and baker. I would look forward to the days she'd bring baked lasagna or cookies into the office. Amanda and I started our banking careers in much the same way in the same company. We came in as tellers and moved up to manage our own branches. When I left the company, she remained devoted to the organization and committed to her employees.

One day, she received a call from the HR department. Amanda was handed a severance package. Her employment termination was effective immediately during the first year of the pandemic.

She was shocked. It took her months to come to terms with what happened. The sudden job loss made her question her worth and decisions. Amanda cried and struggled to get out of bed. After two decades, what she had devoted her time to was all gone. A new director who had the role for less than a year was looking to shake things up. She was part of the shake-out.

Amanda was fortunate to be financially secure enough to deal with her sudden unemployment and the resulting mental and emotional turmoil.

"As secure as I was, it's still scary. Very, very scary," she added.

Amanda shared that her family and friends helped her through the difficult times. They encouraged her to explore her passion for baking. She used her time, which had once been devoted to work time, to learn how to sell through Facebook. She used her skills in business, community building, and managing employees to run Sweet n' Fancy Emporium. Two years after that fateful moment, Amanda now runs a successful business, employing six people. She found Happy Work.

I asked Amanda if she was happy with what she was doing today.

"I am, but yet I miss my career." she replied.

"The career was just a stepping stone to your true profession," I responded.

Sometimes the job you want that takes you in one direction isn't the right path for you. And you might not know it until years later.

WORK IS AN ESSENTIAL PART OF WELLNESS

We've known it specifically as a financial transaction, but work is about being productive, contributing, creating, teamwork, and serving a purpose.

I see myself working in some capacity until I'm unable to; that's the truth. I find enjoyment in creating and producing. It's less about achieving and more about fulfilling my inner desires to give to the world. And I also enjoy the times I get to work and collaborate with others. It's fun working with people who share a passion for a project. It has taken me some time to get to this point, but I hope to help you get here sooner. Here's how work adds to your life.

- **Work offers money.** It is how most people earn a living. We're exchanging time or skills for money. Whether you work for a big company or work for yourself. Your work offers a financial incentive in return for your time and skills.
- **Work offers mental growth.** Your job often challenges you to learn new skills and attain knowledge.
- **Work offers routine.** Studies show routine is good for mental and emotional health and can affect physical wellness, too.[1]
- **Work offers meaning.** You are contributing to achieving a shared goal.
- **Work offers social interaction.** You get to connect with people in the same work situation.

You need some form of work, but it's not the type you've been programmed to do.

How many jobs have you had in your life?

I've worked for 10 different companies. I've had many different jobs. I was a business class lounge server making drinks, washing dishes, and cleaning bathrooms. I may have also carried your bags into the belly of an aircraft. I might have even sold you the wedding ring on your finger. I've been a teller taking your deposits and a customer service rep opening accounts. I've been a supervisor, recruiter, manager, and executive. I started from making $7.00 an hour to earning a six-figure income.

What have I learned? We can work many jobs that don't necessarily have anything to do with one another. But skills, experiences, and networks are all transferable. They can lead to Happy Work.

The knowledge (mental) you learn in one job can help you do another. The experiences you express (emotional) during an interview can be compelling to a future manager, and the network (social) you build can open doors to new opportunities. If you understand how it's all connected, you are empowered to use your strengths to support your occupational health.

"Making plans and having options seems to be at the heart of feeling like you're in control," says Michelle.

Michelle Phan is a Talent Acquisition Business Partner with over 15 years of experience in the recruiting world. She also happens to be a friend. We've had many conversations about balancing work, identity, money, and personal aspirations. She's had many conversations with thousands of job seekers, giving her insights into workers' motivations.

"You will exchange 90,000 hours of your life to work," Michelle said.

A typical 40-hour work week means you will exchange 2,080 hours per year. If you're a 22-year-old recent college grad, you'll need to work until you're 67 to reach retirement age. That's 45 years of 5-day work weeks. And we all know that's on the lighter side. If we included the time it takes to get ready, commute, off-hours work functions, and trips, that's a lot of hours devoted to work.

"No one I'm talking to is looking forward to having to work until retirement," she says. "Being financially free gives you more options with your time, and that can be working or not working."

So, yes, you must rethink how you work.

YOU'RE ABOUT THE RIGHT AGE

Challenge how you view career paths.

Here is an uncomfortable truth: you are not as valuable as you think in your job. You are replaceable. You are not as secure in the career you have. You are a reorganization away from layoff.

You are indispensable, a valued employee, and an important work member *until* you're no longer needed.

"There are plenty of people that are good at their jobs but want to make a career switch, says Michelle. "We're not monochromatic beings with just one area of interest."

"But one thing that holds people back is their financial situation," I said.

"They're almost always locked in, so change is less possible," Michelle added.

"What advice do you share with people seeking new jobs?" I asked.

"You'll have more freedom of choice when your decision isn't solely based on income," she replied.

It's vital that you *work* on your financial health as you work on professional goals.

Having financial security offers you peace of mind to deal with layoffs, allows you to quit toxic workplaces, and enables you to find meaningful work. And there will be a time you simply may want to take time off.

While figuring out things, ensure you take full advantage of all the company benefits offered. Contribute to the 401(k) plans, participate in any stock purchasing programs, and use the tuition reimbursement benefit.

While working hard at your job, continue improving your skills and gaining experience. Do all this to prepare yourself when the opportunity for something better comes your way. And an opportunity for something better will come. You'll have to be prepared for it.

You are very lucky.

I am sure you've been called lucky at one time or another by people who don't see the work you've done to get you where you are. I'm reminded of the quote by Seneca, a Roman philosopher, "Luck is what happens when preparation meets opportunity." Prepare yourself.

I've been called lucky.

I wanted to enter my company's marketing department early in my career. So, I volunteered multiple times to support the marketing department to get experience. At the same time, I took advantage of the tuition reimbursement benefit and went for my MBA. After sharing my desire for the entry-level marketing specialist position, I was told I still didn't have the experience. I wasn't even given the opportunity to apply. And a month later, a recent college grad with no work history got the job. I was the lucky person to open his new checking account.

Suffice it to say, I left the job months later. A year after that slap in the face, some travels, and a quick detour in film school, a wonderful person and board hired me to become VP of marketing. The Norwich MBA, which my previous employer helped pay for, contributed to this opportunity. And my volunteer marketing experience met the new company's objectives. My new CEO said, "You weren't the most polished candidate, but you were the most exciting and passionate."

In the years I worked for the credit union, I used that passion successfully and was offered the opportunity of the successor CEO path. It wasn't luck. It was hard work and determination. And as you've learned, I chose to step away to work on my mental and physical health. That wasn't "luck" either. It was financial security allowing me a different choice.

Be driven by your profession, not loyal to a career.

You'll go through many career paths. Your work goals will change. Accepting that reality can provide you with mental peace. It can open doors for Happy Work as well.

I learned I don't need to be on a single career track. I could work within the financial services industry in a different capacity. To this day, I continue to work with credit unions helping them serve their mission as I serve my purpose.

My former CEO, Christine Petro, is one of my dearest friends, whom I admire as someone who is driven by purpose. She continues to work, saying, "I don't think I'd ever stop, but a break once in a while is good."

That type of thinking led me to conclude that work is essential to well-being, but make it Happy Work.

YOU'RE GROWN ENOUGH TO UNDERSTAND

Work supports financial health, but there's an inverse relationship, too. Financial health can support professional wellness. With money, you can choose the type of work, the company, and the people you work with. Your happy money makes work optional. You can use your time working or on leisure activities.

Bad jobs affect your happiness.

You think you're unhappy because you're not getting paid enough. But you're probably unhappy because the work you do sucks. This leads many to ask for more money to stay in the job they hate instead of figuring out how to make a career move. You can be proactive or wait until the job decides you're not needed.

I have been laid off from a job. I have resigned. And I have sent an email, got up, walked out, and quit. I thought money would solve my dissatisfaction in those jobs. I often did get paid more when I asked, even if it was only a 50-cent raise. The extra happiness bump in hourly pay or the thousands more in salary never did last long. I'd be unhappy in no time.

One day it dawned on me: I am working hard to pay for things to comfort me when I could create a life that needs less comforting.

That changed my relationship to work.

Work supports my financial needs to achieve my dreams, not simply afford my expenses. I also realized something else about working. I needed work in my life to feel productive and connected. The awareness led to a profession where I was paid not for my time or skills but for my experience.

Here's something I want you to understand about work. There's a work hierarchy.

1. A job.
2. A career.
3. A profession.
4. A passion.
5. A purpose.

Your Job

We all start with a job to make money to pay our bills. It's our first relationship to work. It doesn't offer much of anything but a paycheck. And you should earn as much as you can from a job. But you shouldn't get stuck in this stage.

My first job was delivering pizzas. I got a flat $20 for four hours, and all the tips were mine. Some days I made $30, and on good days closer to $100. Luigi would tell me about his passion for making pizzas but encouraged me to find a career. Delivering pizzas was a job. Owning a pizzeria was a passion.

I did eventually find a career in banking and a profession in marketing. All my experiences have led to purposeful work. A healthy relationship with work helped me go from being paid $7 an hour to $5,000 for a 45-minute talk.

Your Career

I want you to start thinking about a career. What work do you actually want to do? This can allow you to explore different career paths. Some companies offer development tracks to expose employees to different departments. If that's not the case, give yourself time to test different careers. This is easier when you don't have significant debt and an expensive lifestyle. So keep that in mind. Control your expenses to allow you to explore Happy Work.

My sister Jennifer started her career as a temp at a pharmaceutical company. She is currently one of the most sought-after project managers in her industry. She said, "It's not about doing everything, but the one thing you do better than anyone else. Companies will pay for that expertise."

Your Profession

Once you discover your ideal career, you want to become the best in it. Be the industry expert that companies are looking for. Why? It comes with a financial perk. You will get paid more for your expertise than for having a broader skill set.

To find Happy Work, cultivate and nurture your work connections— social wellness. A referral from a former coworker is how many people find new positions.

"Remain connected to positive coworkers and bosses through LinkedIn. They can be a source of new work opportunities," Jennifer shared.

And I'll add, praise your connections for their achievements and remember to share your accomplishments too.

Finding Passion and Purpose

I encourage you to take time off. After all, this is Happy Work, where you're empowered to discover more about yourself. It may lead to new skills and opportunities to discover passion projects. And if the passion serves others, you've found yourself purposeful work.

YOU'RE TOO YOUNG TO RETIRE

Don't think of retirement as the end goal.

Let's talk about retirement as it relates to your work. It's the one aspect of working lives that people dream about reaching. But most people don't actually want to retire. They want to do something else with their life. Being financially healthy allows you the freedom to choose to retire.

Retirement isn't an age but a financial number. I encourage people to get their finances healthy, so that work becomes optional. You get to choose the type of work, the people you work with, and the choice to work for yourself.

I actually don't know many people who want to retire. They want to reclaim their work time for *happy time*. They want to do meaningful work.

A study found that 9 out of 10 people were willing to forgo 23% of their future lifetime earnings to do more meaningful work.[2] It's a tell-tale sign that working isn't the problem, considering that housing is the biggest expense taking 21% of income.

Michelle states most job seekers are trying to find work that better aligns with their sense of self.

"I see people leave because of lack of fulfillment," she says, "and they're looking for work that fulfills them."

Work gives us a sense of purpose.

So it's not surprising that we don't just want to quit. We want to do something meaningful. Even people who quit jobs in the Great Resignation didn't stop working. Some started businesses, and others found their way back to old careers.

Work is not only a source of money. It also supports social health and mental growth. And having to get up, get dressed, and participate in a workplace has physical benefits.

"People say they want to be happy at work, and we have conversations about what they want," Michelle said.

"What do they want most?" I asked.

"It's money to have more options, but they want to make an impact, leave a legacy, help others, provide for their family, discover new ideas, and push boundaries," she said.

Think about your current work situation.

How is it benefiting your well-being?

Retirement is simply a transition to something else.

I've shared that retirement is a mindset, not a destination. Many define it as leaving active work life for more leisure. But some have learned it's all about a period of transformation. You regain time to work on other aspects of yourself.

You don't have to wait until you're 70 years old to figure it out. You can do that right now. I encourage you to learn new things to discover your interests. Answer the questions: *what do you want to create? Who do you want to be? How do you want to live?*

YOU'RE NEVER TOO OLD TO REWIRE

You don't actually want to retire; you want to rewire.

Retiring early does sound appealing. There's a group of people who seek financial independence and early retirement. The FIRE community dream of leaving the workforce for more leisurely activities. But I've learned many are still actively working and earning money in some way. Instead of FIRE, I've proposed FINE: financial independence new endeavors. Think rewirement.

1. *Traditional Retirement*

   What most people think about when leaving work life. You work for 40–50 years and retire when you've reached the full retirement age set by the Social Security Administration (SSA) to receive benefits.

2. *Early (Independent) Retirement*

   If you retire before the "full retirement age" set by SSA, you're retiring early. Early retirement is having enough savings or investments that generate income to cover living expenses. You can retire early to explore new opportunities.

3. *Part-time (Working) Retirement*

Having enough assets or passive income streams allows you the option to withdraw from traditional work and use your time as you see fit. But, if you choose to work, you can call yourself semi-retired. This can support social health.

4. *Mini-Retirements (Sabbaticals)*

During a mini-retirement, you'll have financial resources to cover your living expenses. With mini-retirements, you work for a period of years, then "retire" for one or two years before rejoining the workforce again. While working, you would aggressively save money and invest your income to take a mini-retirement or what some professions call a sabbatical.

When I left my last corporate job, I considered it a sabbatical. I encourage others to plan for a mid-career break.

Don't retire; rewire yourself.

People don't actually want to sit around and do nothing. Your life satisfaction and happiness are intrinsically tied to productivity. We are hard-wired to conserve our energy, but we are spiritually inclined to create and produce.

People you've read about in mainstream media who quit high-paying jobs are glamorized. But if you pay close attention, they are ironically hard at work promoting the "retire early" lifestyle on social media.

One influencer privately shared that she's working more hours but enjoying it. "It's not easy, but at least it's meaningful," she said in a chat. The work excites her.

"I talk about retiring early because it's a goal people understand," she shared. "Once their mindset shifts, we can go into what it takes to find meaningful work."

You need to work, and you want to work.

And that's okay to admit. The key to Happy Work is finding what aligns with your values and sense of purpose. The work where you're not looking for the time to hit 5:00 p.m. or for the shift to end. The work where you go, "I can't believe they pay me to do this." And the work that is measured not by dollars and cents but with joy and happiness.

Happy Work doesn't benefit just you.

We are fortunate that there are people driven by professional fulfillment and pushing our society forward. They do research studies, solve world problems, and develop new technology and tools that improve life. Imagine if people were only focused on financial gains. They'd be working on Wall Street, not finding a cure for an illness. But these passionate professionals should also be paid well. We want them focused on solving world problems, not stressing about money.

But there is an issue with overworking.

You can get burnt out doing work you love. There is such a thing as working too much. It's not healthy. Take a break. You have to care for your mental and physical health. And you cannot sacrifice your social and spiritual well-being.

Work is hard-wired into my being. I used to look at success and satisfaction as being based on professional achievements, often at the cost of my health. Whether I was climbing up the corporate ladder or self-employed. I focused too much on work and not enough on other aspects of my wellness.

When my passion projects turned into poison projects, I got sick from working in a profession I love. I realized I didn't set proper boundaries. I needed to use my time for productivity, leisurely activities, and rest. And ensuring I spent time with family and friends, too.

Keep these in mind: being too busy to keep the house clean can lead to stressful home life. Skipping another friend's birthday because of a work function can lead to fewer invitations. And there are only so many times you can miss your child's dance recital until it's no longer a thing they do.

It's about balancing the dimensions.

WORK THE WELLNESS DIMENSIONS

You buy happiness in Happy Work by owning your time. Having the financial means enables you to choose the work you do. You don't have to work but choose to do meaningful work.

Happy Work is about finding productivity that rewards you financially, challenges you mentally, and grows you spiritually. It's work that gives you time for physical health and social connections. It's working in a healthy, supportive workplace that sees you as a human being, not simply a human resource.

You cannot spend all your time on professional success by sacrificing the other parts of yourself. Use the financial rewards of a job to set yourself up to take a break.

What can you do?

Consider looking at your work life. Ask yourself how it's affecting these dimensions in positive and negative ways. Whether you're an employee, a small business owner, a freelancer, or an entrepreneur, understand that you're more than professional achievements—so much more. You can have Happy Work and well-being too.

YOUR HAPPY TO-DO LIST

Use your benefits. Don't forget employers' financial benefits, such as tuition reimbursements, retirement plans, workshops, and seminars. Use them to better your work experience at your current job or in a new company.

Learn new skills. There are many free and affordable online courses on udemy.com, skillshare.com, and coursera.com. Don't forget the specific training offered by Meta, LinkedIn, and Google, too.

Network. Invest time in connecting with other departments. Volunteer in corporate initiatives to meet others. Meetup.com and eventbrite.com are useful networking sites. Explore your interests or find new ones.

Take a Sabbatical Year

In *You Only Live Once*, I introduced the freedom fund—a savings strategy for a sabbatical. A freedom fund supports a year's worth of basic monthly living expenses covering rent, utilities, food, and healthcare.

Your sabbatical is a year for rest and exploration. The time off may open new doors and allow for new skills and new connections that make you healthier and happier.

It can also make you a better employee. I've learned that managers are compelled to work with highly skilled and interesting people. If you don't find this to be true, the company may not be the right fit for you.

The sabbatical year allows your mind a rest from professional goals. But it isn't a time to simply sleep and catch up on housework. You must be learning, experiencing, and proactively doing things. It's a year to pursue interests and work on hobbies and passions.

After a year of sabbatical, you'll find a desire to return to work life with renewed energy and focus.

Many have shared their year-off experiences. Some rejoined their work teams. Others found employment in industries better aligned with their values. A few started their own businesses employing others. And even a handful learned they needed another year to explore.

Until sabbaticals become a company benefit, you'll have to plan for it financially.

CHAPTER 7

Happy Mind

Invest in Yourself and Learn Continually

You can't miss headlines or social posts about mental health. It's often associated with what you're feeling at the moment or your thoughts on what's happening around you. Thoughts and feelings are part of psychological well-being. They are intrinsically tied, seemingly impossible to separate. But there is a difference. And for the purpose of the happy dimensions, you'll explore them separately.

Mental wellness is Happy Mind. It's your intellectual and cognitive ability to process, learn, grow, and use information in a healthy, productive way. You can buy happiness by purchasing knowledge, skills, and experiences. These things improve your mind's understanding and processing capabilities. The more you know, the better equipped your brain will be to deal with unknown life and financial situations. It will lead to reduced stress and more happiness.

"You are not a loan, you are not alone," says Melanie.

"It's challenging to see it any other way when finances are crippling your ability to participate in life," I said.

"Debt is exhausting, and when you have so much of it, your mind can't do anything else but think about it," she said.

Melanie Lockert is the author of *Dear Debt*, a book that helps people break up with debt and become financially free. Melanie had over $81,000 in student loan debt after pursuing her fine arts dream in New York City in 2011.

"The journey has been a rollercoaster," Melanie says, "I've made tough choices to get me from feeling insecure to feeling free. The mental weight of the debt held me back, but I wouldn't let it keep me down."

Melanie was working in a nonprofit with the massive student loan debt taking up room in her mind. At one point, she couldn't afford healthcare and was on welfare. So she left for Portland, Oregon, for a lower cost of living and new opportunities to change her situation.

"I've been paying my student loans for five years and one day decided to see how much was left," she said. "I hadn't made a dent on the balance."

Melanie calculated that she was accruing $11 per day in interest, over $300 per month. The realization caused mental and emotional distress.

"It made me depressed, and I sought low-cost counseling," she said.

An optimistic view of life is a trait shared by people interviewed for my nonscientific happiness study. Regardless of what they were going through, they had a mindset that something better was possible.

"Counseling was great, but I realize I wanted the emotional turmoil to stop," she said. "The only way was to address the underlying issue—the debt."

Melanie searched online for tips and discovered personal finance blogs. There was a community of people sharing their stories: it helped her. In turn, she decided to blog about her debt-free journey as a way not to feel alone, and deardebt.com was born. Melanie wrote letters to her debt as a "cathartic release."

Melanie made $20,000 per year at the time but had minimum expenses. The only way out of debt was to make more money. She started side hustling, everything from pet sitting to delivery and event planning. It was freelance writing that proved to be a game-changer. She made double her annual salary freelancing the first year. And became debt-free four years later.

When I think of someone with a growth mindset, it's Melanie. She was the first to encourage me to do the Road to Financial Wellness in 2015. "Just do it, I'll help," I recall her saying. That was enough to encourage me to take on the challenge of hosting 30 events in 30 states in 30 days.

Melanie's curiosity and love of learning helped her achieve what some consider impossible. She actively and proactively works on money goals while enjoying life. It doesn't mean she has no life challenges, but her mindset, feelings, and money systems lessen the impact.

"Because of being debt-free, earning more, and diligently saving and investing, I have been able to work part-time for months on end and tend to my mental health and physical health. That is so freeing to me," Melanie shared.

IN ALL SERIOUSNESS

I, too, struggled with debt for a very long time. I had a dependency relationship with credit. I depended on credit to fill the gap between my income and lifestyle expenses. I never wanted to pay off the balances because I could afford the minimum payments. And to creditors, I was a good borrower with a high income who paid on time. They showed how valuable I was by rewarding me with higher credit limits.

"There's absolutely nothing we can do," the robotic voice said through the speaker.

"What do you mean there's nothing? I've been a great customer. In all seriousness, I'm experiencing financial difficulties." I pleaded.

"You've had on-time payments," she said, "the system won't allow me to do anything."

"So what are my options?" I asked, holding back tears.

I was overwhelmed with monthly debt payments. My income would no longer cover the ballooning minimums. I calculated my cash flow: I would be in terrible shape within six months. I wanted to get ahead of the issue.

"The system doesn't allow me to make changes to your interest rate or reduce the balance," she said, "you're still in good shape to make payments."

My frustration grew. The customer service rep whom I thought would rescue me from my financial stress only added to my mental distress. I couldn't get my point across: *I can afford the payments right now, but I won't be able to in a few months.*

The call ended with no resolution but a hint that I would need to be in extreme financial distress. Apparently, begging for help wasn't a sign of stress.

That experience with the national bank put my mental and emotional health in crisis mode. I was already feeling the mental stress from having the debt, and realizing I had no options made me depressed. It was debilitating. I couldn't get out of bed most mornings. I began missing work and stopped hanging out with friends. I retreated into my mind, which wasn't a happy place. In the darkness, however, a voice told me to keep going.

The voice I heard was *knowledge*. My exposure to financial knowledge informed my brain that there was a solution. I just didn't know what that would look like. So I researched and learned about debt management plans (DMPs). I reached out to a nonprofit debt management company. They consolidated the credit card debt payments.

Interestingly, the national bank that refused to help me somehow could through the DMP. The nonprofit lowered the interest rate to zero percent, removed fees, and interest accrued, and lowered the monthly payment by 55%. And that three-year repayment plan was paid off in 12 months.

I've thought about that situation through the years. How did I get there? I understood finance, but somehow I continued on a debt-filled path. Debt caused my mental stress, but now I see how my mental health led to my debt situation.

I was struggling with self-love and a lack of feeling worthy. There were negative experiences in childhood that questioned my worthiness. The feelings led to spending as a coping mechanism. I thought I could buy my way to worthiness. And with every credit limit increase, I associated my creditworthiness with my self-worth. It was an unhealthy relationship.

I'm not alone.

I've spoken with hundreds of people through the years who've experienced similar destructive financial habits. They, too, suffered through trauma and abuse. They also understood how to manage money, but their mental health impaired their ability to make sound financial decisions.

"Trauma changes your brain structure," says Dr. Brad Klontz, "you want to survive, so your brain decides to do twists and turns to keep you alive. But some of these things can hurt us."

I spoke with Dr. Brad, a financial psychologist, who shared that "studies found disordered money behaviors like gambling, taking risky investments and compulsive buying is related to a trauma."

We're not alone.

A Money and Mental Health Policy Institute study found that "people experiencing mental health problems are three and a half times more likely to be in problem debt than people without mental health problems (5%)."[1] And the inverse showed that "half (46%) of people in problem debt also have a mental health problem."

Your mental health can impair your judgment in making financial decisions. And your financial situation can cause stress that impairs your mental judgment. It's a doozy. But I know you're making the connection.

"Consider stress as a psychological ability to assess situations," said John Vitug, a doctoral candidate in Applied Behavioral Analysis, "it doesn't necessarily hurt us. It can protect us. But extreme and prolonged stress can lead to cognitive issues."

Being in constant worry over your finances can manifest itself in anxiety, depression, and forgetfulness.

1. **Anxiety:** Feelings that you can't meet financial obligations can become a consistent source of stress impairing your ability to improve financial situations.

2. **Depression:** You can feel trapped in hopelessness over your finances. Focusing on blame over past financial decisions affects motivation to move forward.

3. **Forgetfulness:** Overwhelming feelings that foster the inability to retain information impact your ability to make financial decisions.

Money is a big source of stress for many, causing anxiety and depression.[2] But stress isn't limited to money. People also suffer from work-related stress, relationship issues, medical problems, and social isolation, which are traumatic experiences. The stress you're feeling can lead to bad decisions that create future money problems.

MIND THE MONEY

Money struggles can cause mental health issues, and your mental health issues can cause financial problems.

"Mental health issues impair our ability to think clearly about our situation," John said. He summed up money and the mind:

> One thing I've learned about mental health is that it's not simply about how you're feeling. It is about how your brain is functioning. Some people have brain patterns that impair their ability to make good decisions. People who are experiencing financial stress can often have their mental decision-making capability impaired. So if we can remove the cause of the financial stress, it's quite possible we can let go of the impairment and allow someone to see their situation differently. It can lead to making different life choices.

I can see how mental health can lead to our inability to view money as a tool. It made me think of the self-fulfilling prophecy—a false expectation leads to its confirmation. If I believe I'm bad with money, it leads to making terrible financial decisions. I can then say, "You see, I *am* bad with money."

Financial knowledge changed the trajectory of my life in positive ways. It also did so for Melanie: reaching financial security gives her time. "I can spend [time] on experiences or things that directly impact my health such as therapy, boxing, acupuncture, massage therapy, and coffee out with friends," she said. "It improves the quality of my life."

Invest in yourself by growing your mind. Studies show learning can have positive effects. It gives your brain experiences in which it can perceive the world differently.

How will you grow your knowledge?

GIVE YOUR MIND WHAT IT NEEDS

We go through life being told we must go to school. We do as we're told, excitedly or reluctantly. But somehow, once we finish high school or college, many stop pursuing education and growing their understanding of the world. They stop actively learning.

"We've gone into receiving mode," said John, "we're not seeking knowledge and just accepting information passively, which often supports the mindset and behaviors we actually want to change."

When I said I knew "there was a solution" to my debt, I attribute it to the work I've done in growing my financial knowledge. I've learned through the years that this statement is true: *there is a solution to every financial situation.*

It's an optimistic and positive view of financial situations. Want to invest but don't make a ton of money? The solution is to make smaller investments, as little as $5. Want to lower monthly expenses? You can negotiate a lower payment and keep must-haves in your life. Are you in debt? You have many options and resources to help.

"Your brain can only do what it can do based on its experience and knowledge. So you must expand your knowledge if you want to change your mental capabilities." John said.

Your mindset affects your relationship with money. It's what informs your financial behaviors and habits. Cultivating the right mindset is essential to mental health.

"What are the consequences of thinking that your intelligence or personality is something you can develop, as opposed to something that is a fixed, deep-seated trait?" writes Carol Dweck in *Mindset: The New Psychology of Success.*

The consequence is the realization you have control over your situation. There are many things in the world we cannot control, but money doesn't have to be one of them. We underestimate the role of our mindset in achieving financial milestones, life goals, and happiness.

Dweck, a Stanford University psychologist, coined the terms "fixed mindset" and "growth mindset" to describe underlying beliefs about learning and development. When you have a fixed mindset, you believe you're limited in what you can learn to do or achieve. Applying that to finance can mean you believe that managing money, investing, and creating wealth are impossible.

In contrast, a growth mindset believes you can improve by learning, making an effort, and taking action. You're actively seeking challenges and continually growing through personal improvement. A growth mindset helps you achieve what fixed mindset people believe is impossible—financial independence.

Fixed mindset	Growth mindset
• Avoids challenges • Gives up too soon • Sees effort as useless • Ignores feedback • Feels intimidated by the success of others	• Embraces challenges • Persists in the face of setbacks • Efforts lead to mastery • Learns from criticism • Gets inspiration and finds lessons in the success of others

A growth mindset helps you view challenges and setbacks with opportunity.

At 39, Lindsay Almeida graduated with a masters in business administration. She exemplifies how a growth mindset helps to make better choices for long-term success. Lindsay shared via direct messages that she was emotionally drained and physically exhausted because of her previous employer. "It was a toxic environment," she said, "at times I felt I had no choice because that was the source of my income."

Lindsay shared some alarming experiences at the workplace. One, in particular, stood out. "They make you believe you're not good enough," she recalled, "but simultaneously want you to believe you're only good enough for them." It was causing mental health issues.

But Lindsay had a plan. She leaned into her family and was determined to make a strategic move. Lindsay was tempted to resign when her coworkers began leaving, but she realized it wasn't an option. She needed to make a choice that would also be an example for her daughter, Shelin.

Lindsay said, "Back then, I realized I could be in pain now or in pain longer." She opted for the pain of balancing full-time work, MBA studies, and family obligations. Her growth mindset enabled her to use a company benefit—a $5,250 tuition reimbursement—to help her leave the toxic workplace and get to where she is today.

"I'm really happy where I am," she sent via direct message. Lindsay now works for a company that believes in her and supports her ambitions.

Lindsay contributes a growth mindset to her immigrant roots. She and her mom came from the Philippines for a better life. "Failure was not an option," she said. Their belief in bettering themselves fueled the desire to learn continuously. Lindsay shared a tip, "Don't leave without a plan because you might end up in the same situation or worse."

It's one thing I've learned from my immigrant parents, too. They didn't come to the United States merely to survive; they wanted to strive for something better. And when we came along, they wanted us to thrive. My parents' financial traumas made them messy with money. But they always held a growth mindset. It's a trait that was passed on to me.

My growth mindset has led to better decisions supporting my financial health and overall well-being.

For instance, I declined a gig with a lending company because its values didn't align with mine. The money for a six-month contract was more than the average annual salary for people in the United States. My old self would have taken the money.

But, I learned from a previous bad experience: when I took the money, it led to sleepless nights and lots of stress. I didn't want to go through that experience again.

My Happy Mind knew taking the money would impact my emotional health. It would surely hurt my mental well-being.

Think of your mind as agile and flexible.

You're constantly evolving and changing with a growth mindset. My first yoga teacher, Will Cristobal, said to look at nature for lessons. "The trees that are healthy and alive are moving with the wind. The trees that have died are rigid and inflexible. They'll soon topple over."

You want your brain to be flexible so you don't topple over.

While I believe stress-reducing techniques like yoga, breathwork, and walking are extremely effective, they don't change the brain's cognitive processes. That's where pursuing a growth mindset can help. It can create a new set of beliefs and behaviors. For instance, learning how people become financially free can give your brain a framework to assist you in reaching financial freedom. The axiom is true: you don't know what you don't know. Let your brain know what you want *it* to do.

Do you have a fixed or growth mindset?

Chances are, if you're reading this book, you're in the growth mindset column.

You must make it a priority to learn continually. Not only is it good for your mental health, but it also has financial benefits and supports overall well-being.

MIND THE DIMENSIONS

Invest in yourself: buy happiness in Happy Mind by following your curiosities, learning something new, and gaining experiences. Grow your understanding of the world. Allow your mind to expand. Use your financial health to access knowledge. Go ahead and pay for workshops and sessions that will expose you to new ideas, challenge your thoughts, and improve your mind.

Studies show that learning a new skill and keeping the mind sharp can create a sense of happiness. Consider using your mental capabilities to learn how to improve your physical health or dive into a philosophical study of the spirit. You can discover a new interest and meet interesting people by attending classes. They offer the mental challenges you need and the social interactions you want.

Be mindful of entertainment.

Until my research, I didn't consider how I was being "educated" through video games and entertainment. Finding ways to distract yourself is a good coping technique. But too much of a distraction informs your brain. You are learning something, and it may not be what you want. Some studies I've read claim that video games and movies don't affect people. And, ironically, in those same studies, they'll talk about using video games and entertainment to educate people. I was like, "what?!" If you're going to buy a moment of happiness with an entertaining distraction, be intentional in how you spend your money.

Remaining curious leads to something interesting.

I've learned that my curiosity has allowed me to connect with more people (social health). My yoga practice exposed me to singing bowls, which are made of crystal or metal and vibrate and produce sounds when played. My interest in learning more about singing bowls introduced me to a new friend on the same path who supported my physical and spiritual development. Sharing the journey has been a boost to my mental and emotional health. And interestingly enough, it's led to paid speaking gigs (financial) in some of the most beautiful places (environmental) in the world.

Continually learning supports wellness.

A growth mindset could empower you to learn a new skill leading to a meaningful job with higher pay (financial). You can have a career where you're serving something greater (spiritual). In Happy Work, you can fully express yourself (emotional) and interact with positive coworkers (social). There is a connection between your mind and the happy dimensions.

Choose to learn.

I've met people who stopped learning. They aren't aware they're subconsciously learning from social media, the news, and random conversations. If you aren't proactive in continually learning, you're passively learning to think in a specific way that's unproductive.

What are you watching?

What are you listening to?

What kind of conversations are you having?

If you think it doesn't matter, it does. Your brain continuously processes information, using the data to inform how you see and relate to the world. Be mindful and expose your brain to knowledge that betters your health and wealth.

YOUR HAPPY TO-DO LIST

Learn Continually

Be open to the idea that your mind continues to grow. There are many ways to grow your understanding of yourself and the world. You don't have to attend a formal class or get a degree. But, if that's available, take advantage of it.

- You can grow your mind through books, online courses, workshops, and programs that are offered online, at work, and in your community.
- Curate podcasts and YouTube channels dedicated to educating, not just entertaining.
- Take advantage of your work benefits, sign up for workshops and certification programs, and use the tuition reimbursement benefit.

Research is showing that lifelong learning contributes to happiness. So learning new skills like investing can make you feel happier.

Give Your Mind a Break

Your brain has 6,000 thoughts per day.[3] It's constantly thinking about its place in the world regarding safety and security. The processing is mentally exhausting. You're allowing the brain to rest if you can eliminate certain decisions.

What You Can Do:

- Automate your money
- Set up routines
- Schedule quiet time
- Meditate
- Read for entertainment
- Move your body and go for a walk

Happy Body: Take care of your physical health. You'll need proper rest and relaxation. Lack of sleep leads to brain fog, making it challenging to process what's happening around you.

Happy Work: Your mental health can affect your ability to work, impacting your financial health. It's vital you seek professional help to address mental health issues.

CHAPTER **8**

Happy Heart

Memories Appreciate; Stuff Depreciates

was going to be the owner of a two bedroom and two bath con-
dominium in downtown San Jose. The price tag was $350,000,
which was on the higher end of my budget in 2011.

It was a thrilling feeling to buy my own place. Before I signed,
I caught myself in the mirror, giving me a momentary pause and reflection. I recall wondering if that purchase would solve the emotional
turmoil: the loneliness I felt living in California. Signing the contract
would be the biggest retail therapy purchase ever: I didn't sign.

A few months later, I resigned from my job and used what would
have been the down payment money to travel around the world for
over a year. The somewhat impulsive move to travel rather than own
a home ushered a decade of healing.

My decision did have financial ramifications. The condo I would
have owned is currently worth $1.2 million. Today, I celebrate that
"bad" financial decision of not owning a place in San Jose because it

has led to a happier place in life. I have no regrets. I'm grateful for the path I get to walk. This is my emotional wellness.

How do you respond to your emotions?

Feelings are neither good nor bad.

They can range from fear to joy and from love to stress. Feelings are the perceptions about the world around you. It's an evolutionary advantage alerting us to danger and opportunities.

Dr. Brad Klontz, who co-authored the *Money Mammoth*, said in a discussion with me that we're no longer in immediate danger from a saber-tooth tiger. "Our perceptions must change," he said, "in some ways, we need to reevaluate our understanding of emotions."

Why do some people feel wealthy and others don't? Why do we associate status with luxury cars or designer clothing? Why haven't you asked for the pay raise? Or started investing in the stock market? And perhaps, why isn't more money making you happier? It's the feelings.

Happiness is a feeling.

You can buy happiness in Happy Heart by spending on what truly matters. Emotional wellness is Happy Heart. It's your ability to understand, perceive, manage, and express your emotions and relate with others healthily and productively. Our emotions are the universal experience we all share as human beings. But, emotions are also very misunderstood.

"We are emotional beings, but we are not our emotions," Jonah Kest said during yoga teacher training.

I was in an intense yoga squat, feeling the pain and hoping he'd let us release the pose. But what seemed like hours were merely two minutes. My perception of time was altered because of the physical pain and the emotions I felt.

"I can do it." I whispered. But there was an emotional upheaval happening. I got angry at Jonah. How dare he keep us in this pose? And I got angry at myself, *Why am I struggling with this?*

"Pay attention to those feelings and allow yourself to release them," Jonah repeated.

Those words have helped me embrace my feelings and place them in context. My feelings are not *who* I am but *how* I am doing in a particular situation.

Your feelings are telling you something about your situation too. And if you're unaware of them, those feelings impair you and transfer into different situations.

After a speaking engagement at a corporate event, a mother privately shared an interaction she had with her daughter with me.

One evening she was making dinner for her kids. She was particularly stressed from a deadline at work. Her daughter entered the kitchen and asked, "Mommy, can I tell you something?"

"Not right now," she said.

"But Mommy, I need to tell you something." Her daughter persisted.

"Can't you see I'm busy making dinner?!" she replied harshly.

"I'm sorry, Mommy. I just wanted to give you this," her eight-year-old said.

Her daughter gave her a folded piece of paper with sketches of a mother and daughter. The words read, "I want you to know how much I love you."

The mom's heart sank. She realized her daughter had noticed the stress and was simply trying to brighten her day. It was at that moment she realized the work stress was affecting everyone at home.

The mother and I had a deeper conversation about her stress. We uncovered the financial aspect of that stress. She is the breadwinner of the family. They rely on her income to pay for housing, food, school aftercare, healthcare, and the list goes on. She had to perform well at work not to risk a bad performance review or, worse, lose her job.

The stress was signifying an uncomfortable state of living. The work was stressful, but her finances were major sources of insecurity.

I recommended a strategy that focused on achieving financial security. It would require cutting expenses and allocating money into an emergency savings plan. The goal was to give her a cash cushion to meet financial obligations in the event of an income disruption. Two years later, she shared her improved ability to manage her stress. Being financially secure also gave her the confidence to find a less stressful and higher-paying position.

"Your emotions are telling you something," said John, a Board Certified Behavioral Analyst," Learn to listen to it and address the underlying issue that's triggering these feelings."

MONEY IS FEELINGS

Many financial gurus will shout that money is simply a numbers game. "Do the calculations and follow the math," they'll say. I wish it were truly that simple. Money is more than the paper it's printed on or digits in a banking app. Money is emotional.

But for those of you mathematically inclined, Carl Richards, creator of the Sketchy Guy column in the *New York Times*, drafted an equation: money = feelings.

In 2015, I visited Carl in his office outside Park City, Utah. We had a conversation about money and feelings. He was probably the first guy I met who related money to feelings. It made sense to me at the time. I knew money affected my feelings. However, it would take a few more years to understand the inverse: how my feelings affect my money.

In my travels across the country, I've noticed a commonality in how people spoke about money. It was always with emotion. Whether it was the person crying about her debt, the college grad excited about his first paycheck, or the retirees wondering if they've lived enough in their youth, money was always talked about with feelings.

We know what to do with money: *don't spend what you don't have, use credit sparingly, and invest money*. But our feelings often compel us to do something else. For instance, you know the new car is way above your budget, but it makes you feel something. You know that charging the vacation on the credit card isn't wise, but you do it anyway. You know the dinner bill shouldn't be split evenly, but you don't challenge it. Money is tied up in feelings. Carl wrote in an email:

> If money is all about spreadsheets, how does greed fit in your spreadsheet? How about fear? How about the concern that you're not going to be able to provide the life for your kids that you hoped?
>
> Those are all money issues wrapped in feelings. Or are they feelings wrapped in money issues? Either way, the point still stands. Money = Feelings. Not math."

If money were simply numbers, you could look at bank statements with no fear or joy. It's just numbers. I've seen people's faces light up when they learn their credit score increased by 20 points. Why? The credit score represents access to money (borrowed), so feelings are also associated with it.

If money is feelings, we need to learn to manage our emotions to manage our money.

What emotions come up when money is discussed? What do you feel when friends discuss investments? Is it curiosity or embarrassment? Do you become engaged or withdrawn? How do you feel when bills arrive or an unknown number calls? Can you respond? Or do you feel overwhelmed?

Once you understand that money equals feelings, you can use emotional intelligence (EQ) to improve financial health.

ARE YOU FEELING ME?

You are not your emotions, but they tell you something about your situation.

You align with your values when you realize the people and places that make you feel good. The opposite holds true as well. You're not in alignment when you're in situations that don't feel good.

"Emotional intelligence is your ability to perceive and manage your emotions," John said.

Emotional intelligence heightens your awareness of feelings like sadness. It helps you better manage your emotions. Instead of saying, "This is just how I feel," you look at the situation and environment that creates the emotion. Perhaps, you realize it's your spending or the bad relationship that makes you feel sad.

"It's normal to feel sad about situations," John shared, "but prolonged sadness can lead to difficulty processing information. It can lead to a mental health issue."

Sadness is a feeling, an emotion. It comes and goes, but if your money, relationship, or work continues to make you sad, it can lead to depression—a clinical observable diagnosis. Depression alters how you see and interact with the world.

"When you start having these emotions, you want to understand and address them. It requires looking at the environmental triggers," John said.

It's important to address the triggers and situations that foster these negative emotions. If you're feeling stressed about money, determine what is causing the financial issues, and address them.

My friend and I went for coffee in Jersey City. I couldn't pass up the opportunity to enjoy a cold brew while looking at the New York City skyline. Coming back to the car, we found a parking ticket. The color in my friend's face disappeared as his eyes got bigger. I saw the bead of sweat on his brow.

"How much is it?" I asked.

"$125," he said, handing me the ticket.

My friend started looking at the parking sign. Of course, you must decipher the signs to figure out when to park. I read the last line on the fifth sign, "Residents Parking Only Weekends." You know the frustration if you've tried to find street parking in Jersey City.

I noticed my friend's changed mood. Our great time was spoiled. What was a $10 coffee became the equivalent of an airline ticket to Florida. Having a different financial responsibility, I offered to pay for the ticket.

"Thanks, man," he said with a sigh and a laugh.

It was a good sign. He was laughing and no longer tense. I knew he felt better once he started joking about the situation.

Our finances can stress or comfort us.

I've been financially insecure and know the stress that comes from unexpected bills. It's a feeling I wanted less of. So I became financially secure to lessen those unwanted feelings.

Emotional intelligence (EQ) played a role in my improved financial behaviors.

I used EQ to assess the unwanted feelings. How could I avoid negative emotions? If unexpected bills stress me out, I need a better plan that covers them. For instance, the money in my rainy day fund covered the parking ticket. Money solved the problem. It reduced the amount of time I had to think about it. The stress was cut short. I could freely move on to other things.

How can you use EQ and IQ?

Think of your emotional brain and your logical brain. Your brain wants to protect you, but it doesn't know what it doesn't know. As much as you grow your knowledge (IQ), you must understand your feelings (EQ).

EQ	IQ
Ability to identify, assess, and control the emotions of oneself and others. ▪ Identity, control, and express your emotions. ▪ Perceive and assess others' emotions. ▪ Self-awareness and self-regulation.	Ability to learn, understand, and apply information and knowledge to skills. ▪ Logical reasoning, comprehension, and math skills. ▪ Memory and recall. ▪ Verbal and spatial reasoning.

Source: Adapted from Emotional Intelligence by Daniel Goleman (Random House, 2005).

EMOTIONS ARE YOUR SIXTH SENSE

Emotional wellness means you are aware of your feelings and those of others. You understand that the world affects your moods.

"Emotions are important to understand because they allow us to assess a situation and react for our protection quickly," John said.

Being tuned into your emotions means you'll behave to seek rewarding experiences and avoid unwanted feelings. With higher EQ, you can assess when a feeling is leading you astray or placing you on the right path.

Misunderstood Feelings Lead to Overconsumption

Our emotions are used to manipulate our spending. Pay attention to the commercials you see. It's never about the features but the benefits tied with emotional triggers. For instance, the phrase "You'll look better when you have..." is tied to feeling attractive. If you don't feel good about yourself, you'll be inclined to make the purchase.

Think about the ads you see on YouTube for all the get-rich-quick schemes. Or the social media marketers selling their "secrets to wealth." These people know how to pull your heartstrings and get you to send your *heart*-earned cash to fund the lavish lifestyle they're selling you.

And notice the sales promotions—online, in-store, and by email— are all using emotions: "don't miss out," "everyone already has it," and "big savings." You're more susceptible to psychological marketing tactics when you're unaware of your emotions.

Use Sales Promotions to Your Advantage

Having high emotional intelligence (EQ) and financial knowledge (IQ) can help you save money. My friends have joked about my use of cash rebate apps and discount shopping portals. They think it's a scam and a waste of time. I know the apps are marketing tools designed to affect my shopping, but I use them wisely.

"Don't spend more than you have to," I've told friends. There's nothing sexy about buying an item at full price if you can get it at a discount. The less I spend, the more money I get to keep. I feel great knowing I've spent less and invested more.

With higher EQ, you too can take advantage of sales by buying items you need at a reduced price. The less money you spend, the more you have for financial goals.

Shopping to Cope

Certain emotions can lead you to seek comfort.

When we're stressed about work, relationships, or life, we might shop to feel better. You're stress-buying when you already feel guilt after the purchase. You're stress-buying if you find yourself returning multiple items. You're stress-buying when you haven't opened the Amazon boxes.

Perhaps, it was a challenging day at work, or you had a fight with your partner. Your emotions led you to spend to cope with the issues. And you might have felt a momentary happiness boost.

Retail therapy is an emotional coping strategy. It's a way to gain a sense of control. Small doses can alleviate feelings of overwhelming stress and anxiety. But left unchecked, and as the only way to deal with situations, retail therapy can exacerbate financial issues.

"If we don't look for the actual emotional triggers, we will find ourselves repeating the situation," John said, "and over time, prolonged stress can become a mental health issue. It will begin to impair your cognitive functioning."

I was very close to buying a new car because I was stressed from commuting. I lived 45 minutes away from a previous job. Some days, it would take double the amount of time due to traffic. On an average week, I spent 7.5 hours on the road, which equates to about 30 hours a month commuting. These weren't paid hours. I thought a more comfortable ride would solve my problem. I stopped myself: I decided to live closer instead. It reduced my commute to 15 minutes. Making a different choice eliminated that daily stress and saved me time and money. My savings weren't just in avoiding a new car payment. In fact, a Clever Real Estate survey showed the average worker in the United States spends $8,466 annually on commuting.[1]

Understanding what's causing the stress helps you choose a better response. You want to remove the triggers. Determine how to address your feelings by uncovering situational or environmental causes.

When you have feelings, notice and listen to the emotion. *What are you feeling? Where are the feelings being felt? What led up to the emotions? How is your body reacting?*

Without awareness, retail therapy can become almost the only process your mind uses to deal with uncomfortable feelings. It can lead to financial distress and an inability to walk your life's purpose.

You'll need coping techniques to deal with stress. But use emotional intelligence to find long-term solutions for your life situations.

EXPERIENCES ARE FEELINGS

Memories appreciate and stuff depreciates.

I've learned we buy stuff to buy a feeling. Maybe it's a feeling of control. A feeling of something. But the feeling associated with stuff depreciates. Experiences have a way of paying you back in memory dividends. Spending on experiences is a way to counteract hedonic adaptation. I focus on experiences rather than stuff as a measure of financial success.

Some people value stuff more than experiences. I won't argue with their priorities. I only want to ensure that you're buying stuff that reflects your core values. We associate feelings with stuff so strongly that the storage business is projected to be a $64 billion industry by 2026.[2] We are so emotionally tied to stuff that we can't let it go.

Happiness studies have long found that buying experiences is better than buying stuff. Dr. Brad agrees and shares his equation: experiences > stuff.

I would agree. But stuff and experiences are quite similar. It costs money to have them both. In buying experiences, you don't need money per se, but you need time, which is traded for money. You'll need to own your time to have more experiences.

In 2013, Cristina Valverde did the impossible. She left her Silicon Valley human resource job and moved her entire family to Costa Rica. She envisioned "buying" the same childhood experience for her children. Cristina, 43, was my former HR manager and one of the first to support my company-wide financial wellness initiative. She knew back then about the importance of health and wealth, and the link between money and a happy life.

"We saved as much as we could," Cristina shared, "I grew up in Costa Rica, and I wanted my sons to have that experience. It was wonderful."

Her vision for life wasn't focused on achievements but on a sense of fulfillment. Working in Silicon Valley, you're surrounded by some of the smartest people in the world. They are achieving, but many aren't necessarily feeling fulfilled.

Cristina wanted a better lifestyle and knew her childhood home would make that possible. Moving to another country is never an easy process.

"We got a shipping container and packed it with all our stuff," she said, "There was sentimental value."

After moving back, Cristina realized they had paid to ship stuff they didn't want.

"It was a learning experience. We didn't need much of the stuff we thought we needed. We sold a lot of it," she shared.

Cristina's move was less about geo-arbitrage (living in a lower-cost-of-living country) and much more about giving her children the experience to make them happier adults. But a reality of life is that things don't always go as planned. What would have been a change of lifestyle also came with painful growth.

"I was feeling sick," she explained, "my body was inflamed."

Cristina visited doctors to figure out what was happening. She was given options to take medication but opted for an alternative route.

"My friend said to listen to my body because it's telling me something is wrong," she said, "but I needed to find the actual cause, not just deal with the symptoms."

That led Cristina on an emotional journey of self-reflection. She realized the physical pain stemmed from years of emotional turmoil. Although Cristina was financially secure, other life stresses affected her emotional health, creating an inflamed body environment. It was her financial security and owning multiple businesses that gave her choices. But her emotional intelligence enabled her to make better decisions to improve her life.

Cristina bought herself and her children a different life experience. That's money spent on happiness.

DEBT HURTS

Debt is one of the leading causes of stress. It can lead to mental health issues. The guilt you feel about debt can be debilitating, but you no longer need to be ashamed. You can free yourself of debt's burdens through emotional intelligence.

I want to challenge you.

Pay attention to the emotions that arise when you get the credit card statement. Recognize the feelings debt invokes. Sit with the emotions and explore them. Then, ask yourself: *Why continue using credit? Why are you holding onto the debt? What feelings do you prefer to have?*

Use your emotional understanding to respond differently, which reduces unwanted feelings. Perhaps, it means cutting up the card, calling the creditor, or paying everything off completely. You'll learn more in Book III.

FEELING WORTHY

Your self-worth is not your net worth. Net worth may be the best indicator of financial wealth, but it doesn't equate to worthiness. Chasing the next financial comma may solve money problems, but it isn't going to resolve the nagging feeling that something is missing. The extra financial digit will not replace the lack of connections, relationships, and purpose. There are many examples of people who chase money for emotional highs but continue to struggle psychologically.

Heighten your emotional intelligence. Learn to understand and manage your emotions. Use your desire for positive feelings to make better financial and life decisions.

Feel Your Heart Chambers

We are multifaceted beings; we have many sides to us that make us whole. And some of us come into this world better equipped or talented in one area. If you're high in emotional wellness, lean into your feelings to counterbalance areas that need strengthening.

Your emotional health influences financial decisions that impact other dimensions. For instance, financial anxiety can lead to bad sleeping patterns (physical) and mental health issues. It can lead to mood changes affecting your relationship with family and friends (social). Physical and mental health issues could lead to missing work, resulting in performance issues that will surely impact your finances. It creates more financial anxiety.

You can buy happiness in Happy Heart by filling your heart with experiences. Recognize and manage your feeling with EQ, which can improve your situation or environment. It might mean having a budget, moving away, leaving your partner, or finding a new job. The answers you seek are often felt. Learn to listen to your feelings. They are telling you something is wrong, but it's up to you to respond with emotional intelligence.

What are you feeling?

YOUR HAPPY TO-DO LIST

When you have less financial stress, it empowers you to express yourself fully.

Reflect on the emotional tie you have to things. Stuff depreciates and clutters your mind. Memories appreciate and free your spirit.

Communicate your emotions effectively. You want to be in someone's heart, not on someone's shelf. Invest your time in people and experiences.

Challenge how you experience the world. The world is indeed challenging and tough, but it's also wondrous and beautiful. Optimism and positivity allow me to see the good in situations.

Practice breathwork. Your breath is a link to your nervous system. It responds to your emotions. Pay attention to your breath. When stressed, notice that your breathing is short and shallow. And notice in a restful state that your breathing is deep and long. You can learn techniques to manipulate your breath to control the physiological stress response.

Move your body. The best mood enhancer I've learned for myself is to move my body. Emotions are energy in motion (e-motion). When you're feeling a certain emotion, go into motion to change how you feel. Next time you feel stressed, and you're able-bodied, jump up and down. You'll see how difficult it is not to smile.

Leave five minutes earlier. Leaving the house five minutes early can be enough to avoid bottlenecks on the road: reducing stress. If you can't control rush hour traffic patterns, change when you start your commute.

Learn while commuting. Listen to a podcast or audiobook. Avoid gossip and pop culture shows. They're a good distraction once in a while, but studies show they stir up emotions and can impact mental health. Make the daily commute an opportunity to expand your mind instead.

CHAPTER 9

Happy Body

Be Kind to Your Body; It's Priceless

P rioritize your physical health to enjoy your wealth.

"Your eyeballs are bleeding," my friend Nicole said.

It was a bit of an exaggeration. My eyeballs weren't bleeding, but they were bloodshot. It was another physical sign something was going on in my body. I had just visited a chiropractor for my aching lower back. I was fine, I told myself.

Nicole was concerned. But I laughed it off and replied, "I must have been thinking too hard."

"That's *not* normal," she implored. "Go see a doctor now."

It wasn't normal. I had seen my doctor a few times already. I took all the blood tests. It came back within the acceptable ranges. My doctor said I had signs of stress and fatigue. But I was doing mental gymnastics to avoid acknowledging I was mentally drained and physically exhausted. The frequent episodes of achy joints and lethargy *aren't* normal. Blood vessels bursting in my eyes aren't normal. But even red eyes wouldn't stop me from working. I went into the office with sunglasses and hummed, "I wear my sunglasses indoors."

I recall my doctor at the Stanford hospital saying something along the lines that there is only so much your body can take before you can't take your body anywhere.

She recommended I slow down and find a work-life balance. I had thought I was doing quite fine balancing work and life. Although I admit it often skewed more towards work than life. But I *loved* what I was doing. And I was paid well to do it. Could it really be that bad?

Physical wellness is Happy Body. It comes from having healthy behaviors and daily habits that support your physical body. Physical wellness is your ability to maintain a quality of life without unnecessary fatigue and physical stress.

You can buy happiness by spending time and money on healthy activities. It's about feeling happy in your body.

Sacrificing your physical health isn't Happy Body.

Whether you're working a labor-intensive job or behind a laptop, your body's wear and tear are hard to ignore. You might be able to talk yourself out of mental distress, but it's something else when your physical body can't get out of bed.

I was physically exhausted.

There was aggressive knocking on the door. "We're coming in," said an unrecognizable voice. I was too tired to get up. The doors beeped, and I opened my eyes to two people standing over me. "Are you okay?" one said. I don't recall if I uttered a word.

The next thing I knew, I was lifted onto a gurney and hauled away.

Nicole, who assisted me while traveling, was alerted by the HR manager that I hadn't shown up for my talk. This was atypical behavior. Worried that something had happened, Nicole called the hotel and directed the front desk to get EMS immediately.

I was admitted to the hospital that day for an "unknown" illness. My blood work came back normal. A doctor said I must have caught a travel bug. One of the nurses added, "If we only read your charts, we'd say you're fine, but seeing you in person, you're obviously not fine."

I spent the night at the hospital. Laying in bed, I thought: something really isn't fine.

"If you only focus on making money and don't take care of your mind and body, all that money you're making will just be used to pay for prescriptions you can't pronounce," Patrice has shared.

Patrice Washington is an author and host of the Redefining Wealth Podcast. At 26, Patrice had a multimillion-dollar real estate empire. And then lost it all during the Great Recession. She went from being a millionaire to using SNAP to buy food for her newborn daughter. Leaning into her faith and financial knowledge, she rebuilt herself to seek wisdom, not just education.

I met Patrice on the dance floor at a financial conference in 2013. As we bopped our heads, we began sharing our hopes and dreams. Since then, she's been on world stages, countless online and print interviews, and appeared as the Money Maven for the *Steve Harvey Show*. Patrice used her financial skills to get back into the game teaching others about personal finance. But she knew there was something more than just budgets and credit scores. She wanted others to become wealthy, but not just financially.

"Wealth is not limited to money or material possessions. Its original meaning relates to well-being," Patrice said, referencing the root word of wealth—*to be well*.

When Patrice began listening to her body, she learned the importance of balancing all aspects of herself, from financial goals to professional success to physical health. Today, she spreads wisdom through her six pillars of wealth: fit, people, space, faith, work, and money.

LISTEN TO YOUR BODY

I wasn't listening to my body. Instead, I coped with more fast food, drank, and "conserved my energy" by not exercising. The lack of nutrition, rest, and movement contributed to physical stress. My body was telling me I needed to make major life changes.

My mind was also tired, but it only knew how to keep working. So I pushed through mental distress until my body couldn't keep up. When you don't have the energy to participate in life, it affects your mental and emotional health.

Unable to get out of bed, I had to face the hard truth: I was burnt out. And for someone who associates success with professional achievements, I felt like a failure. If I couldn't work, then who am I? Nicole urged me to use the same drive for success to figure out what was ailing my body.

My job and financial health afforded me access to two doctors. One doctor offered two medications for my symptoms. My Stanford doctor recommended hiking, yoga, sleep, and much less work. I remembered looking at her, confused. How could I be physically active if I'm physically exhausted? Fortunately, I opted for her "cheaper" advice.

My health journey changed from that point on. I RAN to stop feeling rundown. I began to focus on three key areas: rest, activity, and nourishment (RAN).

Rest

We can't be our best selves when we're sick and tired. We can't serve our purpose when we cannot get out of bed.

I allow myself to rest, which includes relaxation and sleep. It's the time allocated for less physical exertion. This allows my body to do what it must to maintain and repair itself. Your body needs to rest. Downtime is essential.

Rest includes meditation for the mind. Your brain is part of the physical body. Don't forget that. Meditation is taking a moment to sit or lie on the floor. Feeling gravity pulling you closer to the ground.

And rest is when you're asleep, allowing the body to focus internally. Sleep isn't limited to nighttime. I encourage short naps too.

Activity

Your body operates with a "use it or lose it" principle. "If you work a muscle, it gets stronger," said Dr. Alyssia. "If you don't exert, move, or find yourself sitting all day, your muscles atrophy. They get weaker."

Your body is built for efficiency. It will conserve resources like muscle tissue if not used. It can result in a reduced ability to move.

I spoke to Dr. Alyssia Pond, founder of ALGYN PT & Yoga, about the importance of physical movement. She said, "Daily movement has a positive effect on every one of our organ systems, from the more obvious musculoskeletal and cardiovascular systems to the regulation of our nervous system."

Movement is vital to our well-being. Our bodies are designed for movement. What tires a physical body is often the lack of activity. You must get up and move for health.

My movement activities aren't focused on external appearances. I want to be physically healthy and feel good. It's an added benefit that my clothes fit better. My three-part routine includes:

1. Stretch and balance for my joints and muscles using yoga
2. Walk and jog for my heart and lungs
3. Resistance and strength training to lift, grip, and move stuff

"Daily movement, even short amounts dispersed throughout the day, can have a profound effect on your life and health," she said.

Dr. Alyssia recommends a daily movement exercise. Just 10 minutes of daily movement. Think of stretching or short yoga practice. Or 20–30 minutes of walking daily, even if every other day, has been proven to be effective.

"You don't have to run marathons to reap the benefits of exercise, and it doesn't have to be costly,'" she said, '"find the movement you enjoy, and do that."

Listen to your body.

There is a difference between good exercise pain and "get me to the doctor" pain when something is physically wrong. You don't want physical pain to become a financial issue.

Nourishment

Think of yourself as an ultra-luxury vehicle. Let's say a Lamborghini. You wouldn't put any fuel type into the car because it'll affect the performance. The same goes for your body. The food you eat is what the body uses to make cells. Give it subpar materials, and it's going to create inferior parts.

As someone who ate just about anything, I finally learned to honor my body by giving it what it needed. I stopped counting calories. I stopped fad diets. And I stopped eating simply because something tasted good. My focus is on nutrition. What does my body need to function well? I listen to my body. Doing so, I discovered certain foods cause eczema and joint pain. I've lived with certain aches, believing they were normal. Knowing how my body reacts to certain foods, I'm very mindful of what I eat. It's not about limiting myself but giving myself nourishment. Focusing on nutrition doesn't mean sacrificing tastes or buying powdered gimmicks. What can you do? Start a 30-day food journal and write down what you eat and how your body responds. It's also recommended to take wellness and allergy tests administered by your doctor. I've done both. Understand what nutrients your body needs and what food is causing issues.

Do you know what's interesting about RAN? It's financially healthy. It doesn't cost much to do healthy things.

STRESS WILL WREAK HAVOC ON YOUR BODY

Many people experience physical stress from labor-intensive jobs. Others experience physical stress due to mental exhaustion—what I call laptop labor. Whatever your job—labor or laptop—both are caused by the lack of rest and relaxation. I was laptop-labor exhausted. I was working 60-hour weeks and traveling to meet aggressive goals. My mind and body were at their limits.

You might think your symptoms are a sign of an illness, but they could very well be a sign of stress. In my case, we ran many tests to find a reason for my symptoms. The test results came back negative. My doctor said, "A no answer is an answer." It meant stress was a culprit.

Stress is a chemical reaction to situations and our environment. As you've learned in Happy Heart, it's natural to feel stress, but chronic stress has a significant health impact. "Chronic stress can affect both our physical and psychological well-being by causing a variety of problems including anxiety, insomnia, muscle pain, high blood pressure and a weakened immune system."[1]

"Stress is one of the main causes of many of our well-known diseases," said Dr. Alyssia, "it puts our nervous system on high alert, which causes a cascade of negative physiological effects over time."

It's essential for you to listen to your body. Pay close attention to the signs of prolonged stress before they impair your physical ability to participate in life.

Effect of chronic stress on the body, mood, and behavior		
On your body	On your mood	On your behavior
Headache	Anxiety	Overeating or undereating
Muscle tension or pain	Restlessness	Angry outbursts
Chest pain	Lack of motivation or focus	Drug or alcohol misuse
Fatigue	Feeling overwhelmed	Tobacco use
Change in sex drive	Irritability or anger	Social withdrawal
Stomach upset	Sadness or depression	Exercising less often
Sleep problems	Increase irritability, anger, and sadness	Withdrawn

Source: Adapted from Mayo Clinic, https://www.mayoclinic.org/healthy-lifestyle/stress-management/in-depth/stress-symptoms/art-20050987.

THE MIND AND BODY CONNECTION

It takes time, but your body will show the wear and tear of your mind. Mental distress manifests itself physically.

Are you feeling tired all the time?

Is it hard to fall asleep at night, but you doze off at odd daytime hours?

There's a good chance you're physically exhausted from mental stress. Your sleep quality affects your mental, physical, and emotional well-being. And research shows that lack of sleep "increases the risk of obesity, heart disease, and infections."[2]

There is a mind–body connection.

"It was 2 a.m.," Michael shared, "I couldn't fall asleep. My mind was racing."

Michael is a good friend I've known for years. He's watched me move from New York City to Palo Alto and go from film school to the executive suite. He was there when I resigned from my job.

"I totally get it now," Michael said.

He was referencing a conversation we had years ago. I was a traveling laptop warrior. It seemed glamorous. Michael didn't understand how I could be physically exhausted staring at a computer.

"So you remember the conversation?" I asked.

"You were mentally drained and physically exhausted," he said.

When Michael moved to the area, his first job was being a restaurant server. But he had big dreams and made bold career moves.

"Back then, I was always on my feet," Michael recounted, "four to six hours of running around, lifting trays, and dealing with customers was physically exhausting. I was tired."

Michael has found professional and financial success working for some of the fastest-growing tech startups. He enjoys his job and finds meaning in shaping employees' workplace experiences. But the work is grueling, often requiring long hours and lots of travel. He began noticing changes in his body.

"But the physical stress from the mental exhaustion is something else," he shared.

Some days he would be mentally drained, unable to keep up with a conversation. Other days he's so tired he can't fall asleep. Not to mention the extra pounds he said he's gained.

"I love what I do," Michael said. "It's demanding work and challenging in good ways, but I didn't realize how much I worked."

Michael has strong social and emotional health. He uses days off to cook for friends and travel. These are good coping techniques but often don't allow for the mind and body to rest.

"Prioritize your health," I said, "if not, all the money you make will be used to pay for future treatments and medicine, not future travels and meals."

The wildest thing about physical burnout from mental exhaustion is that we can't wrap our minds around why we were physically tired from staring at a laptop. So we do more, not less.

Your mind is an organ called the brain.

It's a physical part of your body. Research shows our brain needs rest, too. Give your brain the rest it deserves. Meditation works, but you can also use movement to reduce mental stress.

THE HUSTLE AND GRIND BODY

When I started my entrepreneurial path, I fell for the hustle trap. I couldn't escape the culture. Everywhere I went, people exclaimed about the virtue of "sleeping when you're dead." Many proudly bragged about working 24 hours without sleep. Some even posted about skipping meals and family gatherings just to "make dreams happen."

The hustle culture promised financial rewards. I used to call it the Gary Vee effect. Gary Vaynerchuk is a business mogul and media personality. He is known for his hustle-centric motivational sermons. It was his in-your-face Jersey-toned lectures that drew me to him initially. He felt familiar. I'd listen to Gary late at night to keep myself motivated. But one day, I watched a video and got sick to my stomach. My body was physically reacting to the message. It wasn't Gary Vee per se. It was the hustle culture of sacrificing our mental and physical health for professional and financial gains.

Fortunately, my heightened mental awareness alerted me to the pattern I was repeating. This time I chose my physical health.

Many of the people in the startup entrepreneurial world have had a change of heart, too. We all collectively realized that you couldn't function and be productive without sleep. The goal of any business is profitability and longevity. How sustainable can a business become if the founders are too sick to see its vision through? Times have changed for the good. I know Gary Vee has changed his tone as well. He encourages people to sleep and spend time with family.

So, I want you to rest, relax, and sleep.

I believe in the seasonality of effort. You can hustle and grind, but only for a time. Gears that grind for too long get worn out and then thrown out. Don't throw out your body for the sake of reaching financial goals. You have to be healthy to enjoy wealth.

MONEY MOVEMENTS

There's a financial connection to physical health.

Being healthy supports wealth. Your physical wellness can support financial health. Having fewer health issues reduces medical bills. When I was hospitalized for my mysterious illness, I received medical invoices for an entire year from doctors I didn't know I met and services I didn't know I'd had.

Another financial benefit: people who are healthier often live longer. You're giving investments more time to grow. You will reap the benefits of compounding with a longer time span.

SPEND TO GIVE YOURSELF A BREAK

How many hours have you spent mowing the lawn, cleaning the house, or running errands? You've worked all week and find yourself working through the weekend. No wonder you're exhausted on Monday.

Use the money to pay for help around the house.

Instead of spending four hours mowing the lawn, pay someone $50 to do it for you. You now have four hours to sleep and exercise.

My sister Janice has a career in legal and compliance. Her work duties and three daughters keep her quite busy. My sister gets groceries delivered because shopping can be stressful. "I'm willing to pay for the service," she said. Janice shared she saves money because the kids aren't asking to buy stuff or place items in the cart.

But the biggest benefit, she says, "is the time savings." She doesn't have to get the kids ready, drive to the store, and shop the aisles. The extra minutes saved allow her to sit still, close her eyes for a bit, and just relax. And she often finds herself walking around the neighborhood. It's done wonders for her health, she said.

Paying for services and help can be worth the expense.

Here's a calculation to figure it out: take your hourly pay (or divide your salary by 2,080 to get your hourly rate) and compare that to the cost of hiring help. If you're making $25 per hour, and it costs $15 for a delivery charge that saves you two hours, the math works out to *saving time and money.*

BUY FOR HEALTH

My two German friends asked me, "Why do Americans wear gym clothes everywhere?" I hadn't noticed this until they pointed it out.

In fact, athleisure wear is expected to grow to a $153 billion industry.[3] We spend a lot of money to look like we're working out.

Instead, buy items that make it easier to do healthy activities. I love to walk, and having comfortable shoes makes it more enjoyable. The right bed is worth the expense, but it doesn't have to be an expensive mattress. You'll come to realize there are really only a few things you need.

It's paramount to use money for wellness. Spend on healthy activities and proper nutrition. Be willing to pay for apps and trainers that motivate you to do exercises.

Remember this: money might help you afford better medicine and doctors, but it won't guarantee the best health. Money can pay for healthier food, fitness trainers, and equipment, but it still requires you to show up and do the work daily.

YOU ONLY HAVE ONE

We only have one body. And we're stuck with it until some biotech genius finds a way to get us new bodies. Even if it were available today, it would be unaffordable to most people. That leaves us with one option: take care of our current body.

"You only live once," Susan exclaimed.

I laughed and excitedly said, "That's the title of my first book."

Susan and Michael Chavez were a couple I met on my 21-day cruise in the Caribbean. We hiked to "touch the Pitons" in St. Lucia. As we sat eating, Susan shared how Michael retired early. Both worked for utility companies and weren't high-earning executives. Susan shared how they saved and invested but knew it was important to enjoy life. It was noticeable on the Norwegian Cruise ship we were on. They were the life of the party.

"I'll tell you something, Jason," Michael said, "the older you get, the harder it is to do things physically. Take care of your body."

I've noticed that for myself. My body doesn't move as it used to. It's one of the reasons I have a movement practice that includes walking, yoga, and balancing routines.

As we finished our meal, I asked, "When money isn't an issue, what is the secret to a happier life?"

Both Michael and Susan said it was about balance. They enjoy retirement, spend a good amount of time connecting with friends, and are physically active.

"You have to keep moving," Michael shared, "it keeps the mind and body healthy."

Listening to your body is vital to your physical and financial health.

Pay attention to what it's saying: the aches, pains, and tiredness. Allow your brain to rest from all the mental processing. Don't sacrifice your body for materialistic gains. Use money mindfully to support your physical wellness. You need your body to enjoy your wins and wealth. And remember these three words: rest, activity, and nourishment.

You can buy happiness by spending your time on physical health.

A Happy Body means being active, hydrated, nourished, and well rested. You're feeling good. It boosts your energy and confidence. You're mentally alert and physically able to work on projects and socially interact.

Prioritize your physical health to enjoy life well into retirement. You want to live long enough to enjoy the gains from your 401(k)s. And you want to be physically healthy so you can spend your money on enjoyment, not treatment.

There is no guarantee your body will be able to do what you want later in life. It's about balance in living today and planning to be around tomorrow. But in the meantime, take care of your body; it's priceless.

How will you honor your body?

YOUR HAPPY TO-DO LIST

Get Proper Nutrition

Focus on getting nutrients into your body. You don't have to sacrifice taste, but it requires training your taste buds to enjoy less salt and sugar.

Drink More Water

You're not drinking enough water to hydrate your body and mind. My doctor said dehydration is often a cause of headaches, cramping, and muscle pain. Taking her advice, I drink, on average, 100 ounces of water a day. I have noticed the difference.

Create Work–Life Boundaries

This doesn't mean that you try to balance work and life each day. You want clear boundaries for when you work. Create a schedule for intense focus and light work. Don't check work emails or messaging apps after you've clocked out. Use your weekends, holidays, and paid time off to rest, relax, and reset.

Meditate

Your mental health will affect your physical body. I've found meditation to be an effective tool to lower my anxiety. Meditation can be a 60-second practice or a full-hour lunch session. Give yourself a few mental breaks throughout the day.

Sleep More

It goes without saying that you need more sleep. I refer to 30-SUP (stop using phones), which is mindfully not checking the phone 30 minutes before bed and 30 minutes after waking up. Turn off the notifications. And keep the smartphone away from your bedside.

Read a physical book, which usually does the trick for me. For environmental wellness, I don't have a television in my bedroom. My sleep space is my sanctuary. I've trained my body and mind to immediately relax upon entering the bedroom.

Move

We lose our flexibility as we get older. It's much more important to remain flexible and agile. Get up and do some light stretching. Start with your head all the way down to your toes. Go for a walk twice a day. Health experts recommend 10,000 steps. Start with 1,000 and challenge yourself to break your record steps.

Don't Avoid the Doctors

Get routine physical checkups. You want baseline health vitals to compare to future checkups. Have a conversation with your doctor about your wellness goals.

CHAPTER 10

Happy Social

Connections Are Your Lifeline

onnections are invaluable. You must cultivate and nurture them. The pandemic has taught many of us about the importance of healthy relationships. It's increased the necessary discussion about social health and its impact on well-being.

Social wellness is Happy Social. It's your sense of belonging. Your ability to genuinely engage with others in a meaningful way. You're fostering healthy and supportive relationships with people around you—at home, at work, and in the community. Happy Social is buying happiness by investing time in others. You are consciously aware of the importance of connections and social life.

We are social beings, and we need interactions to feel well.

There is a lot of value in our relationships with family, friends, and colleagues. I don't think we consciously know how important relationships are to our happiness. We make time for things we value: know the real value of relationships and make time for them.

My family and friends have enriched my life.

They've made happy moments possible. We've laughed, cried, had deep conversations, and had silly adventures. And they've helped me during challenging times. They were my support in the darkest of moments. When I was financially struggling, they offered compassion and couches. My friends even took me out for coffee and paid for movie tickets. "I know you'll get me next time," my best friend once said. And sure enough, there were times when I got him.

As I started reconnecting with family and friends in person, they all shared how much their respective inner circle helped them during social distancing. When the world was falling apart, and fear was growing, they leaned into their relationships and created "social bubbles" to help them through quarantine. They emerged much better than others who found themselves in complete isolation and desperation.

There are examples of people who have different sets of priorities. We can learn from their stories. One reader shared his story:

> Before COVID [BC], I was boasting about saving a few dollars not hanging out with friends. I gladly told them my financial goals were a top priority. My friends would still invite me for drinks. Probably hoping I'd eventually come. I was committed to reaching my financial independence goal. They just didn't understand how important it was to be financially free. They didn't get it, but I didn't care. Then the pandemic hit, and no one asked me to hang out because we couldn't. I don't think I would have gone anyway. As days turned months, I was getting angst. In BC, saying no to a social gathering gave me control. I don't have control now. I'm miserable. I can't believe I chose to skip hanging with friends to save $20. I feel so alone.

He isn't alone. I've met others who chose financial goals over family and friends. Stories of people not attending weddings, skipping out on birthdays and social events to aggressively pursue their financial independence goals. "To what end?" I would ask them.

A research study has shown "potentially serious mental and physical health consequences" among older adults who "have experienced an acute, severe sense of social isolation and loneliness."[1]

I don't fit the study's demographics, but I did feel the impact of isolation too. The study differentiated the difference between the feeling of loneliness and the frequency of social interaction. You need to interact with others.

Before the pandemic, many self-proclaimed money experts chastised people for choosing friends over finance. Online "gurus" proclaimed the virtues of skipping social gatherings to reach goals. And guess what? These gurus gained a lesson about choice. It's better to choose *meaningful* relationships than chase money goals.

There's a particular story that sticks with me.

A 20-something dropped his friends for financial independence. He told everyone that his "sacrifice will be worth it." Well, eventually, his girlfriend left him, and invitations from friends stopped.

"It was rough losing my girlfriend, but my best friend telling me that we weren't friends was a special kind of tough," he said. He realized too late that not being involved in the friendship meant there was no friendship.

Don't chase money and sacrifice your relationships. You can buy many things with money, but you can't buy deep, meaningful connections. You cannot replace lost time with money.

If there's one thing I've learned from wealthy people and older adults, you can go bankrupt, but with the right friends, you won't be broke for long. Cultivate your inner circle for your well-being.

CULTIVATING YOUR INNER CIRCLE

Happy social is a healthy connection of giving and supporting one another. It's essential to wellness.

Studies have shown that social connections might help protect your health and lengthen life. "Scientists are finding that our links to others can have powerful effects on our health. Whether with family, friends, neighbors, romantic partners, or others, social connections can influence our biology and well-being."[2]

The axiom rings true: you are who you surround yourself with.

Who are you then?

You Are Who You're Intimate With

Work on yourself to be the best you can be. The person you'll spend the most time with is you. Spend on growing your knowledge, improving your health, and getting to know yourself intimately. Become the person that attracts the right partner. Otherwise, we pick the partner that's "good" right now, not the person who's good long term.

Your partner can affect your health.

A recent study by Japanese researchers analyzed nearly 35,000 long-term couples and discovered similar blood levels, cholesterol, and triglyceride. The couples were also more likely to experience similar health issues from diabetes to hypertension.[3] Long-term couples become biologically similar. The finding echoes a 2016 study by University of Michigan researchers showing similarities in kidney function, cholesterol, strength, and depression. The study looked at blood test markers of over 1,500 older couples and found biological synchronization.

Not only do you start looking like your partner, but your actual biology transforms. And if you're both suffering from health issues, much of your worries will be around medical bills.

Your partner can affect your wealth.

Have a partner who aligns with your vision and financial goals. You have to see eye to eye with the finances. Otherwise, an extreme deficit in the financial dimension will impact your social connection. Financial issues are a leading cause of divorce. It might be you or your partner's bad financial habits that are causing the issues. Being financially healthy allows you both to be your best selves. Instead of arguing all the time about money, you're spending time creating your dream life.

There are ways to navigate tough financial conversations with partners. Erin Lowry, the author of the *Broke Millennial*, shared during my event at the Financial Gym in New York City that "we must get financially naked with our significant others."

Her advice is to communicate. Be honest and upfront about your money situation. Share the financial messiness and successes. Express your goals and dreams too. And with heightened emotional intelligence, you can respond with understanding and empathy to move forward together. Erin does caution about toxic relationships that often lead to financial abuse. "Know the signs and seek professional help," she said.

You Are Your Family and Friends

They love you for who you are, not how much you have. Family and friends do care about your well-being. And they want you to be stress-free. If you're experiencing less financial distress, you can be yourself and be more present with them.

Friends and family care about you.

When I hit financial rock bottom, I was scared of judgment. Some in the financial space did have remarks, but my family and friends gave support. It placed everything into perspective. I've learned the people who are *fixated* on your credit score and investment portfolio won't miss you when you're gone. The people who will miss you are the people who saw past the finance and saw the friend. Your healthy connections won't judge you because you've failed. They want to know how to help you succeed.

Some of my early success was supported by friends with big dreams too. My first speaking gig was offered by my friend Melba. She wanted me to share my story with her team at a nonprofit. Melba opened the speaking gig doors for me. And it was through a friend and MyFabFinance founder, Tonya Rapley, that I got my first $5,000 speaking gig.

Coworker friends are necessary.

My friend shared that being a new teacher was challenging. Leo wasn't quite sure if it was going to work out. He shared that making friends at work helped him through the first year. "They guided me and gave me space to vent my frustrations," he said. "They knew what it was like and encouraged me to keep going."

Leo leaned into his social health and cultivated a social life at work to counterbalance the stressful job. Coworkers understand the demands at work more than anyone else. Having friends at work makes challenging jobs much better.

You Are Your Healthy Connections

It's vital to nurture healthy relationships and invest time in them. But relationships aren't limited to your partner, friends, and family.

You can have healthy online friendships.

My online connections have helped me accomplish impossible goals. It was a network of bloggers and social media friends who banded together and offered their time to support my financial literacy efforts.

And you can have healthy work connections too.

I got my first credit union job because a coworker, Marcia Waithe, asked me to join her when she left the bank. The friendly gesture changed the trajectory of my banking career. Working at my first credit union is where I met my late friend Nicole. She took me from the teller line during my first month and made me an assistant manager.

Your work relationships aren't limited to coworkers.

Mark Cochran and David Snodgrass were executives I connected with during my time as a lowly branch manager. And both are now CEOs of two of the largest credit unions in the country. When I pitched my financial wellness road trip, they were the first to support me enthusiastically.

Your social circle needs age diversity.

My first book, *You Only Live Once*, was made possible because of a friendship with a credit union member. Marge and George Alexander would visit the branch bi-weekly for the latest interest rates. We'd have fun conversations as I helped them with savings strategies. I've also been over for home-cooked meals. The friendship remained even after I left the company. Years later, when Marge read my Facebook post about wanting to be an author, she messaged, offering her support. Her son, Fred, connected me to my first editor at Wiley.

Many people lose out on the joy of having intergenerational friendships. Marge and George were 30 years older than me. Sometimes you meet people, and it's an instant connection.

A healthy social network lessens worries and can help you do amazing things. They aren't a drain on your wallet and don't impede your progress. Unhealthy connections, however, add stress and hold you back.

You Are Who You Avoid, Too

Some people bring drama and negativity with every encounter. You will need to curate them out of your life. It can be tough because of history and a sense of obligation. But, cutting ties to improve your social health might be necessary.

First, you don't need to remain connected to people who enable your bad habits. They only see you for what you were, not who you're becoming. You'll recognize these people who comment against your progress and question your ambitions. Do what you can to avoid them.

Second, you don't have to get along with every family member. Stop trying to appease everyone. Have healthy boundaries with family. "Just because there's blood doesn't mean there is a bond," a therapist said during a workshop.

I've heard family members question my life choices. They simply didn't understand my ambitions, but they made sure I heard their opinions. I learned to set boundaries. I limited interaction with the negative relatives and engaged more with the supportive family.

Last, avoid drama-filled coworkers with endless issues. They bring negativity into the workplace. They might be a fun distraction at first, but they often fosters a toxic work environment. Their social drama impacts your wellness. The negativity can influence your attitude about work, causing performance issues and financial impact.

I intentionally avoided work drama. It made some coworkers think I was boring. I focused on developing relationships with managers instead. Here's advice: make the negative coworkers think you're boring. They'll leave you alone eventually. You can then focus on positive coworkers who teach new skills and support your career ambitions.

SOCIAL DYNAMICS OF MONEY

Your financial health allows you to set boundaries.

Having money enables you to leave abusive relationships and toxic family members. I encourage you to get your financial life in order. You might not be financially independent, but you can become less dependent on others for your financial needs. Be mindful of the influence of others that affect your finances, too.

Keeping Up with the Joneses

Are you buying things and spending because everyone else is doing it?

If so, you're trying to keep up with the Joneses. I'm not quite sure if the phrase still applies, but the meaning behind the words is still relevant. Trying to keep up with the spending of your social circle will only lead to living a life you don't even recognize.

A surprising study found the neighbors of lottery winners are more likely to file bankruptcy. The study showed "that people who lived near big lottery winners had larger holdings of visible assets like cars, motorcycles, and houses, suggesting that their conspicuous consumption may have been what got them into trouble."[4]

Most people aren't aware of how others affect their spending. Perhaps, you were like most people, but now you know better. Your connections are affecting your financial health.

If you're looking for a financial role model, look to those who spend their money wisely. These people may not live in the biggest houses, drive the nicest cars, or take exotic vacations. Rather, they have minimal debt and adequate emergency savings. Most important, they're content with what they have and how much they earn and don't feel the need to keep up with anyone.

A Night Out with Friends

Happy Social is about managing conflicts while showing respect for yourself and others.

One evening I was out to dinner with a group of 30 people, only a handful of whom I knew. Because of the familiar situation, I proactively asked the server for a separate check. She respected that I was on a budget.

When the bill came, a few guys started shouting to split the bill evenly. The loudest among the group yelled for my portion of the bill. He wanted me to pay $150. I stated my bill for the salad and beer had already been paid. He demanded that I pay "my fair share" of the bill. I'm not sure who said it, but someone shouted, "You're cheap, man," followed by laughter.

I got up, looked at everyone, and said, "I'm not cheap. Cheap is ordering everything on the menu, drinking excessively, and expecting someone else to pay for it."

Later that evening, a few people from that dinner group approached me. They said it was a good lesson on how to navigate "splitting the bill evenly." One shared the challenges of friendship and financial goals. "It doesn't have to be black and white," I said, "but your friends should respect your financial health."

Splitting the bill isn't the best approach. Some friends will always eat and drink more. It rarely evens out.

People spend based on habit.

If you're a frugal spender, you typically spend less. But spendthrift friends will rarely curtail spending to fit your budget. And if you continue splitting the bill evenly, you're simply subsidizing their lifestyle. It's an unhealthy friendship with a slight hint of financial abuse.

Sacrificing your financial health to fit into a social group isn't social wellness. Happy Social is about open and honest communication with friends. You are supportive of each other's goals.

Connections in Times of Need

Rita-Soledad Fernández Paulino was having an autoimmune response to stress. In 2019, her doctors recommended six months of medical leave. Soledad, a public school teacher, had to budget money for the first time with a reduced salary. When her husband's business closed, it pushed their family finances even further to their limits.

"It was a stressful time dealing with my physical health," said Soledad, "but then we had to juggle financial issues, too."

On bed rest, she found support from family and friends. A cousin shared his budget and introduced her to personal finance books. She devoured the information. It took her mind off the physical illness and mental distress.

"They were a source of strength for me," she said.

Soledad had a supportive inner circle. Her friends would come to visit and ask what help she needed. "Please get me personal finance books," she said to them. The support from family and friends during that time changed the trajectory of Soledad's life.

"The financial knowledge helped me balance the budget, pay off medical debt, and have money to find a healer," she replied.

Soledad was able to use the time to expand her mind (Happy Mind), heal from trauma (Happy Heart), and improve her finances (Happy Money). The experience has led to meaningful work (Happy Work). Soledad founded Wealth Para Todos to coach others and support underrepresented communities on their health and wealth journey.

Belonging to a Community

Taking care of one another is a form of self-care. In contrast, focusing on yourself and the loneliness that follows is unhappiness. Happy Social is about supportive communities and your role within them.

John and David Auten-Schneider are the Debt Free Guys™.

I met the married couple back in 2015 at my Denver event. Their mission is to help the gay community achieve financial well-being. On the debtfreeguys.com website, the duo admits they "were the gay cliché of living fabulous but being fabulously broke."

"I grew up feeling like I didn't belong, and finding a community where I belonged was freeing," said David.

John and David credit the community that led to acceptance and belonging.

"When you've found love and support from others, you want to offer it back, too," David shared. "We wanted a place for social gatherings and where friends could stay close to nature."

"We were looking at property in the mountains to build a vacation home, and we could barely afford our current lifestyle," John added.

They both knew how important friendships were to happiness, but their finances were hurting. David and John had $51,000 in combined credit card debt. Sitting in their basement apartment tallying up their debt was an "aha moment," they said.

"We felt we had to keep up the lifestyle," said John, "It led to depending on credit cards."

They wanted to talk about their debt. But it's a conversation not many have within the gay community.

"I remember when we came out to our families and friends about our debt, everyone started opening up," John said.

Friends began sharing their finances too.

John and David found ways to support friendships and financial goals. They offered alternatives to expensive dinners and lavish weekend getaways.

"We invited friends to the park and took advantage of things like museums during free admission days," David said.

"We came up with fun and frugal ways to spend time with friends," John shared with pride.

I love it when people find frugal ways to enjoy living life. It's not about deprivation, but finding an affordable way to remain connected with others. Frugal isn't about being cheap. It's about being intentional with money.

When David and John accepted their financial reality, they made different choices that resulted in financial independence. The Debt Free Guys™ exemplify the importance of community to social wellness. And the responsibility to give, as much as one gets, to support a community's health.

YOUR SOCIAL HEALTH IS SOCIAL WEALTH

Develop meaningful connections.

Surround yourself with people who push you forward, listen to your concerns, and offer encouragement (emotional). Friends who support healthy activities (physical), share new experiences (environmental), and respect your financial goals. Seek out coworkers who introduce new books, concepts, and ideas to grow your mind. And get close to family who want you to succeed professionally. Surround yourself with people who inspire you (spiritual).

Your greatest wealth is your connections.

Buy happiness by investing in people. Happy Social is about meaningful connections and having a social life. Connections are your lifelines, and studies show social connections are what make people happier.[5]

Social wealth is built over time, similar to financial wealth. The more time you give to healthy relationships, the more opportunity for healthy returns. While many connections are assets, some are liabilities. Be aware of your social circle's influence over your finances and overall health. Mind the conversations that encourage you to do unhealthy things and spend way above your means. Don't filter friends solely based on money, either. Some friends may be bad with money but are kind, generous, and loving spirits. Perhaps, it's your influence that can help them.

Your network is your net worth.

What is your network saying about you?

YOUR HAPPY TO-DO LIST

Nurture Relationships

Have meaningful conversations with friends. Send messages and notes that nurture friendships. Make it a habit to connect in the good times, not just in times of need.

Spend on Loved Ones

Treat your loved ones to coffee, dinner, or a movie. It's called prosocial spending. Studies continue to show that spending money on others contributes to happiness more than simply earning more.[6]

Set Boundaries for Balance

Don't let your social activities hurt other dimensions. Hanging out with friends all the time can affect your work performance, financial health, and physical well-being. There is a time and place for social interactions.

Cultivate Friendships

Ensure that you're creating meaningful connections with others that are supportive and positive. Make intergenerational friendships too. I love connecting with older adults with a vast array of life experiences. And having younger friends reminds me to look at the world with fresh eyes and curiosity.

Curate Your Feedships

Your social media friends have an effect on your happiness and well-being. Be mindful of the online access you give people to your life. The wrong access often leads to emotional and mental distress. Social media is a great communication tool but also a big distraction.

Participation Awards

Don't be a spectator in your friends' lives. Participate in real life. Find opportunities to change a passive relationship into an active, meaningful friendship.

Join a Club or Association

Explore an interest and find groups that offer knowledge, resources, and community. Not only will you learn and support your growth mindset, but you'll also meet like-minded people for friendships.

Neighborly Connections

Having neighborhood friends adds to a healthy home environment. My neighbors have helped water plants, take care of pets, and pick up the mail when I've traveled. And I do the same for them.

Community Involvement

Get involved in your community. Advocate for the social programs that benefit you and others. Attend events sponsored by community leaders and elected officials.

Don't Lend Money to Family or Friends

Avoid lending money to people because it often affects relationships. You can give money to family and friends if you can afford it and don't want to be repaid.

Support Your Friend's Business

Buy a copy of their book, download a music track, shop their online store, order a cake, share their business, or invest as a silent business owner. With that said, supporting a friend doesn't mean you need to be their salesperson or buy into a business scheme.

CHAPTER 11

Happy Space

Free Your Space and Yourself

Free yourself from the messiness of your desk, clutter in your home, neighborhood blight, and community limitations. Design your environment to support your happiness and well-being.

How livable are the areas you physically inhabit? Do they inspire or cause you to perspire?

I lived in a loft apartment downtown. It was close to the airport and a train station to New York City. I've always wanted to have big windows and open spaces. But I didn't realize how the environment was affecting my health.

"Are you all right?" Franklin asked.

I had friends over when a series of emergency vehicle sirens passed the apartment building. It caused my body to tense up. My friends noticed how uncomfortable I became.

I was affected by the city's sounds, including honking cars, crowd noises, sirens, and gunshots. It was a constant reminder the neighborhood wasn't the right fit. Even after several car break-ins and unsavory encounters, I reassured myself it was okay. But I wasn't okay.

Environment affects our mood. And research "has shown that our physical environments significantly influence our cognition, emotions, and behavior, affecting our decision-making and relationships with others."[1]

It's possible the environment impaired my decision-making, causing me to stay longer than I needed to. Your financial health should give you options to buy into the neighborhoods that make you feel safe and live in homes that allow you to rest.

Environmental wellness is Happy Space. It's the physical environments where you live, work, and interact. You're living in spaces supporting inner peace, safety, health, and connection. Happy Spaces include your home, office, neighborhood, community, and the world.

Your financial health gives you the option to own a home.

During the pandemic, my friend Franklin closed on his first house. He'd been living in a small studio apartment with his family to save money as they paid off their student loan debt. Franklin did dream about home ownership, but he was listening to a financial personality advising people not to buy homes unless you paid in cash and were debt free. However, Franklin's family of four was outgrowing the tight living space, with a new baby on the way. So, he went against the personality's advice and instead listened to our conversations on holistic wellness.

Franklin was prepared: he worked two jobs, downgraded his car, and did side hustles that allowed him to buy a home. Franklin bought happiness by upgrading his living space. He spent months working on the home to create a Happy Space. He said being able to customize the home to fit their needs was the "best investment for his inner peace and family's security."

Franklin did the financial calculations, but he determined the home's impact on his mental, occupational, and social health were the deciding factors.

Housing is the biggest expense for most people concerning environmental wellness. Making decisions that don't factor in other happy dimensions can profoundly impact well-being. You might find yourself further away from work, family, and friends impacting your mental and social health.

You can do the math to determine where to live and whether buying or renting makes sense. However, I want you to think about housing differently.

Filter the decision to rent or buy based on its effect on your wellness dimensions. Consider these questions: *Does owning a home support your psychological health? Is your home near parks and recreational areas for physical activities? Are you closer to work? Will it be easier to socialize with family and friends? Is the environment clean and the neighborhood safe?*

Marianne Scarzello is a human resource director at Tucson Old Pueblo Credit Union. She bought a home in 2019 after years as a renter. After an event, Marianne asked if I thought a house was an investment.

"A home isn't a financial investment. It's a place you live, a necessary expense," I replied.

"People say renting is a waste of money," she shared.

"Owning can be an investment giving you returns that aren't financial," I said, "renting isn't a waste of money either. It's a different type of housing expense."

"I think it's an opportunity to settle in and make a home," Marianne said.

"Yes, look at homeownership as an opportunity to create your Happy Space," I emphasized.

"I got a new roof, chimney fixed, solar panels, some electrics, bathroom leaks are taken care of," she shared.

After three years of ownership, Marianne still hasn't painted, focusing her attention on home repairs. And she emphasized, "It was well worth it." Being a homeowner allows her to create a Happy Space.

When you find the neighborhood you want to live in, it can be good for you to invest in that community. Owning a home gives you a connection and a vested interest in the neighborhood. You might even find yourself more involved with local issues.

Should you rent or own?

The answer largely depends on your finances and life goals. I have seen different calculations to favor one over another. It's widely shared among money experts that the cost to rent a place is the "roof" of your housing expense. In contrast, the mortgage on a house is the "floor" of your housing costs. When the furnace breaks in your apartment, it's covered by the landlord. If it breaks in your home, that's an expense you'll need to cover.

Renting does have its benefits: it offers more flexibility. You can test out neighborhoods and change your environment easily. Although you don't build equity, you have less responsibility for maintenance and repairs.

Decide whether settling down in a particular area is part of your life plan.

Your primary home is an investment in your peace of mind. Owning allows you to build equity, but there's no investment return until you've sold it: you'll still need a place to live. Owning does offer more stability without wondering if your lease will be renewed. And most importantly, owning gives you the option to customize the house into your dream home.

Housing costs vary significantly based on the area you choose to live in. Whether you rent or own a place, it must support your well-being: it must be a Happy Space.

Are you inhabiting Happy Spaces?

YOUR HOME SPACE

A happy home space is a healthy and positive place to live, rest, and enjoy.

"Your home is a reflection of you. Ask yourself, 'how do I want my home to look, feel, smell so that I am happy in my space?'" said Dorethia, founder of #MoneyChat.

Dorethia Kelly is a friend and CEO of Work·Space·Spark, an online community for working professionals. Her former career in healthcare finance and operations included designing facilities. She shared the importance of green spaces, music, and bright environments that foster positive emotions. Dorethia states there is a link between the physical space and people's morale and productivity.

"When you have spaces that are neat, clean, and fit your personality," said Dorethia, "it definitely improves your mood and overall well-being."

Take a moment to look at the spaces you inhabit.

Start with the room you're currently in, expand to the entire home, walk around the neighborhood, and drive around town.

What thoughts and feelings are you having? Are you happy? Is your space clean? Do you feel safe? Does it offer you easy access to what you need?

I'm all for making any place you live—rent or own—a Happy Space. You don't have to spend much to make your home happy either.

What is your home saying about you?

Clutter Is Messing with You

Start with the physical objects that are already in your home.

Studies have shown clutter can affect your well-being. Clutter is "defined as an overabundance of possessions that collectively create chaotic and disorderly living spaces."[2]

"It doesn't allow us to think when we have clutter all around us," said Dorethia.

"It creates a feeling of overwhelmingness, and instead of getting things done, we tend to procrastinate," she added.

The environment we create around us can indicate what's happening in our heads. "A cluttered space can mean a cluttered mind," my mentor once said. During my chaotic years, my place was disorderly, never messy, but cluttered.

"Clutter has a profound effect on our self-esteem and our moods."[3] A UCLA study of 32 families found a link between clutter and high cortisol (stress hormone) levels. The study shared that people felt more anxious looking at cluttered rooms or piles of paper.

I feel anxious when I'm in a cluttered space. I have heightened alert. My brain is trying to determine if there are any threats in the clutter. I also feel unmotivated when I'm in spaces with too much stuff.

A study at Princeton found clutter competes for the brain's processing capabilities.[4] In many ways, the brain tries to keep track of objects and use cognitive resources. "The more objects in the visual field, the harder the brain has to work to filter them out, causing it to tire over time and reducing its ability to function."[5] So if you're feeling tired in a cluttered house or unproductive in a cluttered desk, you'll want to clean the environment.

Declutter your space.

Help your mental health and remove unused and unwanted stuff.

1. Create decluttering piles: keep, trash, sell, and give away.

2. Set small goals for yourself—a drawer, a closet, a room—rather than trying to finish your entire house or apartment in one day.

3. Emptying a room lets you see how much stuff you have and how much storage space.

4. Mind the emotional "buts" when decluttering. "But it was a gift," "but I paid money," or "but it reminds me of." The "but" items are often forgotten until it's time to declutter.

5. Sell your items and fund your savings goals.

A Clean and Organized Space

My brother Jeffrey has always been meticulous regarding his stuff. His home is a reflection of that trait.

"I like an orderly, clean home," Jeffrey said.

He even tells guests to squeegee the bath tiles after showering. I've done so myself when visiting.

"We've worked really hard to own a home. If we maintain the house, we'll spend less trying to fix it up later," he shared.

His house is also designed for functionality, minimalism, and flow. It's not overly packed with furniture or with excessive decorations. But the home is still warm and inviting. Jeffrey's home is an example of a Happy Space—a clutter-free home.

"We don't want too much stuff," he said, "I like to have what's essential."

Buying less stuff means there's more money to fund savings goals. But if you have unwanted stuff, you can make money too. Jeffrey shared that he doesn't throw away stuff. He sells the used items online, "We know other people want to save money and the stuff doesn't end up in the landfill."

You can declutter your space, help the environment, and get back some of your money.

Have you ever done an inventory of stuff in your house?

Everything you see can be represented in money. Either you bought it yourself, or it was given to you, and even if you found it on the side of the road, someone paid for it.

Is there stuff you can sell or give away?

Create Separate Functional Areas

Happy Space isn't about minimalism. It's about living with your essentials. You want a space that has your personality and offers what you need. You'll realize it doesn't require much and is good for your financial health.

Walk around your home.

Is it representative of who you are? Is it functional? Do you have a favorite area? Where do you feel most productive? Where do you feel most relaxed?

Consider creating spaces for the following:

- A space for lounging
- A space for entertaining
- A space for rest
- A space for working

Can you identify any of these spaces in your home?

"You want clearly defined spaces," Dorethia said, "I highly recommend that you try not to put your home office in your bedroom because it can cause stress if things are hectic."

Your bedroom must be a sanctuary. You don't want to be reminded about work while in your bedroom. You want a space where you can rest and rejuvenate.

I understand many don't have the physical space. I lived in a 400-square-foot apartment in New York City. I learned clever ways to make use of tiny spaces. It's going to take creativity.

Dorethia recommends getting "a small room divider" so that when you're done working, "You can place it in front of your work area to have some separation of work and downtime." And there are lots of books and videos available on this topic. It doesn't cost much either.

Your Workspace

Your physical work environment affects your health and productivity.

Is it an inviting place to work? Is the space stuffy or open? Is it bright or dull? Does it have amenities to support productivity? How is your workstation set up? Is your desk cluttered?

Take stock of the physical work environment. And share your thoughts with your manager on how to make the office functionally happier. You'll be surprised at how productive you become. It may even help you score a better pay raise.

I've worked in dark and dreary office buildings with harsh fluorescent lighting. It was an uninviting environment. In one company, they had stacks of boxes all over the office. I felt lost in a maze of boxes. Was a coworker going to surprise me around the dimly lit corner? It was not an environment that fostered creativity.

Some companies have attempted to improve the workplace with varying degrees of success.

One friend shared he enjoyed going to work when they remodeled the office and added a relaxation room. He said it showed the company encouraged healthy breaks throughout the workday. Another friend said her work performance decreased when the office moved to an open floor plan. She couldn't concentrate with the added noise and distractions. And a reader shared his sentiment about hot-desk policies where you can "choose your desk" and move around. It "sounded great at first" but created anxiety.

You may not have control over the general design of your office, but you can make your desk or work area more pleasant.

Dorethia said to surround yourself with things you love. "Place those things in your workspace. Whether it's a picture of a fun vacation or figurine, you found at your favorite thrift store, put it within eyesight each day."

Some people work from home, which means design and functionality apply to your work-from-home office, too.

Dedicate a Workstation at Home

Many people work from home but don't have dedicated desks or offices. Dining rooms, kitchen tables, and bedrooms have become offices. Work is creeping into designated areas for rest and entertainment. You must not sacrifice your physical and mental health.

"Avoid having the remnants of your job or business in all areas of your home as this can be a constant reminder of your to-do list," shared Dorethia, "and can cause you to work more instead of having set boundaries."

Your brain likes patterns, and it'll begin to recognize your bed as a workstation. So, if you're having difficulty sleeping, you'll need to stop working from bed. No laptops, no tablets, or smartphones to answer work emails on your bed and in your bedroom.

Create a workspace in your home.

It can be a corner area of a room. Find the right furniture that fits into the space. If it's inside your bedroom or common living area, choose a desk that can easily hide work-related items after each work day. Help your mind switch from work to home.

Create an extended workspace outdoors.

Take advantage of beautiful weather and work outside. I switch from my home office to working on the patio. Having the flexibility keeps my mind alert and body moving when working from home.

YOUR DIGITAL SPACES

Your digital environment is messing with you and affecting your finances. Your desktops and smartphones are digital spaces you inhabit.

Let go of the browser tabs.

You think it's the best way to keep organized, but having 30 tabs open is just using up your laptop's processing power, in much the way the clutter on your desk is using up your brain's resources. Do yourself a favor, bookmark tabs, and remove them from your visual field. And while you're at it, remove all the downloads and files from your desktop.

Delete the emails.

My friend was showing me a photo on her phone. I noticed the red dot on the mail app: it indicated over 15,000 unread emails. I wanted to comment, but I noticed I had 2,000+ unread emails myself.

Declutter your inbox.

Unsubscribe to email subscriptions and marketing emails. Not only will having an empty inbox improve your mental health, but you'll also spend less, too.

Clean-app your smartphone.

I bought a "welcome" mat for my front door. That seemingly mundane purchase made me think about my phone. Once I enter my password, what am I seeing?

You don't need all those apps. Delete unused apps and download them again when necessary. Categorize them based on functionality. Group all finance apps under "money" and social media apps under "distractions." And while you're at it, choose an awesome, inspiring photo as your background and screensaver. So every time you enter your digital space, you're reminded of what's important.

Your social media feeds are virtual environments.

One of the best pieces of advice I received was from a 78-year-old man's take on social media. He said to be careful of who we "invite into our house." Our social media connections are digital house guests. They occupy a virtual space and impact our health.

He asked, "Do you really need to know what an acquaintance or coworker thinks about the news?" It's true: scrolling through our digital space, we see a lot of "nonsense." It does affect us.

Take a moment to think about your digital environments.

Is it helpful and inspiring? Does it allow for meaningful engagement? Are you learning? Or do you find yourself sad, angry, and distracted?

Digital cleaning supports your financial health.

When you clean your digital spaces, you're less susceptible to marketing tactics and social influencers selling you the latest needless things. And, if you didn't know, "social influencer" is a marketing term. It's used to identify people who can influence the sale of stuff. So, yes, social influencers are just salespeople.

How many salespeople do you really need to be connected to?

YOUR OUTDOOR SPACES

The neighborhood affects your mood.

Are the streets clean? Do you feel safe walking around? Are the homes in the block well kept? Is there a good ratio of concrete to greenery?

Michael and Charles were excited to become first-time homeowners. But after a few months of living in the neighborhood, they realized how anxious it made them feel. They live in a beautiful home in the San Francisco Bay Area. They love their city, but the neighborhood has been less than desirable.

"We come home from a work trip or vacation feeling good, then we see what we're returning to, and we immediately feel stressed," Michael shared.

Michael realized the neighborhood was impacting his mental health.

"We spend time cleaning the street and bagging garbage," he said

This was a daily occurrence when I've come to visit.

There was also an instance of an abandoned car with busted windows and no wheels parked in front of their house. After repeated phone calls, the city still hadn't removed it. Fortunately, they have good neighbors (social health) and lean on one another to counterbalance the neighborhood issues. And they take advantage of the Bay Area's many outdoor spaces.

Find your ideal neighborhood that supports your well-being. Get involved with your neighbors to improve environmental and social health.

Extend your living spaces.

Enjoy open spaces and parks in your community. Go for a walk and experience the outdoors. Notice what's all around you. It can give you a momentary pause on a stressful day. It can give you the necessary motion for your body. Getting into natural places can elevate your mood.

The Color Green Is Good for You

Green is more than the color of money. We see more green hues than any other color. Some say it's a biological adaptation to differentiate food sources or easily spot plants in sparse areas.

"One way to balance any space is to have plants," said Dorethia, "they have a subtle way of elevating your mood."

And the mood-enhancing benefit is backed by science. Researchers state that green is in the middle of the color spectrum. Our eyes don't have to strain much, allowing the nervous system to relax. It's why our mind associates green with calmness.

Go on a forest bath and relax.

Look for a place with trees. Immerse yourself in the experience. You're not exercising. You are using a Japanese technique called *shinrin-yoku*—bathing in the forest atmosphere. Some studies show the health benefits of forest bathing and immersing yourself in green. It can "bring you into the present moment and de-stress and relax you."[6] It's a financially healthy coping technique.

SAVING MONEY AND THE ENVIRONMENT

Watch your consumption. It affects the environment and your finances.

There's a financial benefit to thinking about the environment. Using less energy, water, and gasoline reduces your monthly expenses.

Turn it off. Unplug electronics, turn off lights, and keep the thermostat 1–3 degrees lower to reduce energy consumption.

Save water. Don't shower for too long. And don't let the faucet run while brushing your teeth or when shaving and washing dishes.

Bike and walk. Use an alternative to driving your car for local trips to save on gas. An added benefit is improved physical health.

Use a water bottle. It's helped me drink more water while reducing my use of single-use plastic bottles. And it saves money.

Buy clothes you'll wear multiple times. Avoid fast fashion that's priced very cheap but causes you to buy more. It is financially and environmentally unhealthy.

Keep your electronics longer. There are a lot of rare minerals in our tech gadgets, and we're destroying ecosystems to mine them. Eco-waste is toxic. How were we programmed to believe a $1,000 phone should last one to two years? Break the tech cycle.

SPACES AND DIMENSIONS

Buy your happiness by investing in spaces that support your well-being. You can optimize your space for mental health and social interactions, carving out areas for meditation and entertaining.

Money can affect your environmental wellness. Your financial health gives you options to live in your preferred neighborhood or to customize your home for rest, entertainment, and productivity. If you have the financial means, don't feel guilty hiring help to clean your house or the yard. You don't have to do everything yourself to achieve the Happy Space you desire.

And the reverse is true: your environmental health can affect your money. Cluttered homes, unsafe neighborhoods, and long commutes are stressful and impact your health. It can lead to mood changes, medical issues, and lost productivity.

Your environmental wellness is Happy Space.

Choose an environment where you feel safe, rested, and creative. How much better can you think (mental) and express yourselves to others (emotional)? Your improved moods can motivate you to exercise (physical). Your home can be a place to host family and friends (social). It might also offer a space to create (occupational) and connect with your higher self (spiritual).

How will you invest to improve your space?

YOUR HAPPY TO-DO LIST

Design your environment to support your happiness and well-being.

Declutter your home. Go through each room of the house separately.

Mind the sounds. Pay attention to the sounds you hear throughout the day. The noisy refrigerator or hissing cooling system is affecting you. It's worth the expense to have them fixed. Play mood-enhancing music throughout your home.

Move to change your mood. Go out for a walk. Sometimes our work and home space cause stress. Changing your scenery can help you gather your thoughts in a new environment.

Fix little nuisances. Studies show little annoyances around the house build up stress. The leaky faucet, the squeaking door, and the unhung photo all occupy your mind. Write a list of all the little nuisances in your home. Spend a weekend tackling them.

Take a digital detox. Take a vacation from social media for 30 days. Get into the physical world and reconnect with friends offline. You'll find improvements in your psychological, physical, and social health.

Clear your mailbox. Opt out of prescreened marketing offers. Under the Fair Credit Reporting Act (FCRA), creditors or insurers can access credit reports to make firm offers that are not initiated by you. Visit www.OptOutPrescreen.com.

Reduce unwanted calls. Add your phone numbers to the Do Not Call registry to prevent telemarketing calls. However, other types of organizations may still call you, such as charities, political groups, debt collectors, and surveys. Visit www.DoNotCall.gov.

CHAPTER **12**

Happy Spirit

Serve a Purpose, Not a Purchase

Y ou don't always have to do things for financial return.

There is more to life than money gains and material accumulation. I'm sure a financial guru is huffing in disapproval right now. But that's not you: there's something more than the monetary system we've been indoctrinated under.

Spiritual wellness is Happy Spirit.

I'm referring to the values and beliefs that provide a sense of meaning and purpose to your life. The Happy Spirit dimension is where your actions align with your values, you're serving your purpose, and you've connected to something greater. All in the spirit of creating in this world. You buy happiness by giving to yourself and others.

I won't get religiously dogmatic or New Age spiritual.

Spiritual wellness is the inner motivation, fire, and desire to be our best selves and to serve. Improving your spiritual health can lead to more joy and happiness.

"Do you think there's something more?" Tiffany asked.

"I have to believe there is more than the rat race we're all in," I replied, "otherwise what is the point in all this?"

"It's about fulfillment. I have this sense of peace and enoughness. I'm whole," Tiffany replied.

Tiffany Aliche, the Budgetnista, is a good friend and author of *Get Good with Money*. I've seen her "overnight success" that was 10 years in the making. She's dedicated her life to educating women to catch their dreams.

Most people don't know about Tiffany's story, about how she moved from being broke to becoming whole. At 26 years old, she had a teaching career, owned a home, and balanced her budget. However, during the Great Recession, she lost it all: her job, relationship, and home. Tiffany was also a victim of credit card fraud, leaving her with $35,000 in debt. At 30, she moved back home with her parents and retreated away from her social circle. She had lost all motivation until a dear friend reminded her that financial problems had a solution. Tiffany used her financial knowledge and improved her situation. After doing so, she vowed to help others avoid financial mistakes and pain. She found her purpose.

Tiffany has supported me since the beginning of my journey. We've aligned in so many ways, and she continues to inspire me. Her determination, service, and resilience can only be best described as a Happy Spirit.

"How do you know you're fulfilled?" she asked.

I didn't reply immediately.

Thousands of thoughts passed through my mind. I thought about the stages I was on, the places I visited, the big money I was paid, and the awards I received. I am grateful for those moments, but I have wondered about an alternative life.

"If I'll be honest with you, Tiffany," I said, "I was achieving, but I wasn't fulfilled. I had this nagging feeling something was missing. I started with a purpose, got pulled into the race, and then forgot where I was going."

"What got you here isn't going to get you there. Learn to let go," she said.

That's exactly what I did in the last three years. I let go of expectations, influence, and achievements. It's brought me acceptance, enoughness, and fulfillment. It didn't curb my desire to do work. It had the opposite effect. I've felt more inspired to create and give. I truly feel connected to something greater.

SOMETHING IS MISSING

Have you felt this nagging feeling that something is missing?

You cannot escape the news of celebrities who seem to have it all publicly and suffer privately. Famous people who are surrounded by adoring fans. They are doing financially well, look physically great, are mentally sharp, emotionally expressive, and live in the comforts of their homes in wealthy neighborhoods. Yet, something is still missing. They feel an emptiness that cannot be filled. It's a spiritual crisis. The stress from the crisis often leads to self-medicating and problematic behaviors. The results of these actions become a distraction from dealing with the spiritual void.

You've heard these stories before, but it's not an issue exclusively for celebrities. I have felt this void. The feelings that something is missing. It's difficult to conceptualize and harder still to communicate.

You know the emotion: the nagging feeling there is something more to life. You've had the thoughts, the unrelenting questioning of your pursuit of professional and financial goals.

Without addressing this void, you succumb to the same celebrity temptations to suppress your thoughts and feelings. This leads to decisions that create problems that later become your distractions.

ARE YOU SEARCHING FOR A PURCHASE?

We're taught to consume our feelings away. It's led to spending time searching for a purchase rather than finding our purpose.

We consume to fill an emptiness that only leaves us feeling emptier. And somehow, we've learned to believe we just haven't found the right purchase to fill the void. So, we consume some more. And if there isn't enough money, we exchange more time for money to buy more. Even without cash, we'll use credit to buy a little more. It leads to overconsumption, financial stress, and spiritual deprivation.

"We know there is a void, and we do all these other things," says Weslia. "We sex it, drink it, drug it, we do all these things to the point we'll deplete our resources to fill that void."

"Many do chase money to buy things to fill that void, resulting in more exhaustion and dissatisfaction," I replied.

"All we need is to stop and allow our innermost being to be fulfilled," added Willa.

Willa Williams and Weslia Echols are Accredited Financial Counselors (AFC®) and hosts of The Abundant Living podcast. I was a guest on their show, where they have spiritually minded conversations about money, faith, and living a fulfilled life.

"I've used shopping as my coping technique, but I was never able to buy fulfillment," I shared.

"Peace and joy, family, make people happy, not stuff," Willa replied.

"It's never enough with stuff," Weslia emphasized.

I've seen people buy things, then buy shelves to put things, then buy boxes to organize things, then move things into basements, attics, and garages. And sometimes, people buy storage units to store their things.

Stuff and things represent your time.

You *are* those things that are boxed, stored, and forgotten. No wonder you are feeling something missing—*your time.*

Time is your most valuable resource.

It's as intangible as the concept of spirit. But we can *feel* both the passage of time and the growth of spirit. Some philosophers say the spirit is the force by which time flows. When time is exchanged for money to buy stuff, it's possible you've also exchanged your spirit.

So, experiences are better than stuff, right? It's vital to understand there are similarities.

I want you to look at the self-care industry. It's valued at $450 billion.[1] The industry promises you happiness through experiential consumption. You can fill that void by caring for yourself through experiences. Spend on the massage, the facial, the candles, subscribe to meditation apps, indulge in luxurious retreats, and so on. I actually like these things for myself. It's important that we take care of ourselves. But, I've learned these purchases aren't the answer to filling the spiritual void.

We are metaphorically exhausted from bucket lists. We're literally suffocating from stuff and figuratively burying our spirit. We continue on a cycle of earning and buying. It all ends with the same result: spending more time finding something to buy rather than finding what makes us feel alive.

"Find how to give to others—you'll find wholeness," Tiffany said.

GIVING BACK TO SERVE A PURPOSE

A growing number of scientific studies are leading researchers to connect giving to happiness.[2] You can interrupt the "earn and buy stuff" cycle by giving to others. Give your time to family and friends, a cause, a project, a community, and a purpose. You're investing in people by giving with no calculation of return.

I've allocated 10% of my annual income to causes that align with my values. I support entrepreneurs (kiva.org) and artists who create (indiegogo.com). I also financially support initiatives and programs helping underserved communities.

But giving back isn't limited to money, I give my time to worthy causes such as serving in advisory councils, as a mentor to college students, and as a nonprofit board member. I can see how my donation of time and money positively affects people and organizations. Giving back boosts my mood.

I heard an ancient Chinese proverb years ago:

If you want happiness for an hour, take a nap. If you want happiness for a day, go fishing. If you want happiness for a year, inherit a fortune. If you want happiness for a lifetime, help somebody.

I learned the importance of giving by watching my mother. She gives whenever she can. My mom sends money to family in the Philippines and will give money to a homeless person on the street. When my best friend's childhood home burned, she donated to support the repairs despite living on a fixed income herself. My mom said, "if you can help someone, why not help? It makes me happy."

How do you feel when you've helped someone?

Giving is a trait of an abundance mindset.

When you believe there is enough in a world created with abundance, you have more than enough for yourself and everyone else.

Weslia and Willa shared that giving back is aligning money with spirit.

"When you live in abundance, you're tapped into your spirit," Weslia said.

The abundance mindset is the belief that there are enough resources for everyone. And we can share our resources with others.

"Your spirit only knows abundance," Weslia added. "It's when we have a scarcity mindset we are going against ourselves."

The scarcity mindset is the belief there is never enough time or money. It affects how you view and live in the world and interact with others. Scarcity causes you to behave in ways that impede happiness.

"How can we live in abundance and fill the void?" I asked.

"We have a responsibility for ourselves, and we have a responsibility for others," Willa replied.

Willa shared that she gives 10% of her income too. She doesn't focus on the 10% that's been given but practices gratitude for the 90% that remains.

"There is always more than I need and more than enough left to share and give to others. Giving to others gives me pleasure," she added.

Studies have shown giving has an emotional return. Experiments show evidence that altruism is hardwired in the brain – and it's pleasurable.[3]

Giving can give you a sense of purpose.

Do you give back? Or perhaps, will you give back?

YOUR PATH TO PURPOSE

Living a life with no purpose is why you might feel unfulfilled and think it's all hopeless. Purpose is serving something greater than yourself. It can be your family, kids, community, or a cause.

I've recognized a process that's helped me and many others find purpose.

1. Identify your core values (awareness).
2. Explore your curiosities (interests).
3. Devote time and energy (passion).
4. Discover how it serves others (purpose).

Identify Your Core Values

They are fundamental beliefs that act like principles that guide behavior. Values are unique to each person. They can be personal qualities, relationships, and material things. They can come from childhood experiences, cultural and societal norms, and values passed on by parents. They can also come from marketing on social media.

"Our values are our spiritual core," says Willa, "we have to do the work to understand what drives us to set the right financial and life goals."

I used to set goals because society or marketing tried to convince me about what was important. After clarifying my core values, I realized some goals took me away from my purpose. For example, my money goals caused me to chase higher-paying jobs, not purposeful work. In one instance, I became a subprime mortgage broker because it paid high commissions. The misalignment caused a great deal of distress. I lasted 30 days in that job.

Knowing your core values allows you to focus your time and effort. You're choosing happiness when activities align with them.

To identify your values, you must answer the question: *what matters in your life?*

Ask yourself why these things matter to you. For example, why is family important? What does family provide you? Your list of things that matter to you can and will be different from others. Settle on three or four values.

Some things that matter in your life might include:

- Wealth—the means to live in comfort
- Family—a feeling of belonging
- Relationship—intimacy
- Education—knowledge increases opportunities
- Travel—experiences bring joy
- Health—physically fit
- Work—contribution

There's no right or wrong when it comes to values. The key is knowing which values you operate from and using that awareness to guide you.

Your values will change over time as you achieve life milestones and gain new experiences. This often results in your purpose evolving as well.

Explore Your Curiosities (Interests)

Connect your interests to your core values.

For example, an interest in the Grand Canyon is connected to the core value of travel. An interest in investing is aligned with the core value of wealth. Interest in meditation is aligned with the core value of balance.

Start with your core values if you're having trouble recognizing your interests. Think about the things that align with them. If your core value is excellence, you might attend workshops or enroll in classes to increase your knowledge.

My core value of health led me to explore yoga after being introduced to the practice at work.

If you haven't identified your core values, at the very least, write down your interests. And if you don't know what you're interested in, I challenge you to get out there and explore. Gaining experiences can introduce you to new interests. Put yourself into unique situations with an open mind. You'll recognize this challenge as an attribute of a growth mindset in the Happy Mind dimension.

Devote Time and Energy (Passion)

Once you've discovered interests, devote time and energy to them. Doing so turns the interest into a passion. Passion is simply what you devote your time and energy to.

I enjoy yoga. I have a daily practice that helps me with my flexibility and mindfulness. I am healthier, which allows me to serve to my full capacity. Yoga is a practice I devote my time and energy to. It's a passion.

Passions do come and go.

Your time and energy will shift into other things. What I have learned is knowing my core values often realign me. There was a period when I stopped my yoga practice to chase professional goals. I was burning out. When I reaffirmed my core value of health, I shifted my time and energy back into yoga. It's how I became a certified yoga teacher. Interestingly enough, pursuing my certification introduced me to breathwork—another one of my passions.

There will be moments when you're passionate about something. You will allocate most of your time and energy to pursuing your passion. When you decide to no longer devote time or energy to your interest, it's no longer a passion. And that's okay. You might have outgrown the interest, which no longer aligns with your core values.

Discover How It Serves Others (Purpose)

When your passions serve you and can serve others, you've found purpose—serving something greater than yourself.

My passion for yoga has spilled into my financial wellness mission. I regularly incorporate yoga movements and breathwork into financial discussions. It has helped differentiate my approach and aligns two core values—health and education.

Perhaps, your passion for investing has led to teaching others how to get started. My friend Jully-Alma Taveras is the Investing Latina. She started investing when she was 19 years old by contributing to her company's 401(k) plan. Jully's interest became a passion. She immersed herself in learning everything about investing. Years later, Jully started an Instagram account educating others on how to invest. Her unique style and approach have attracted tens of thousands of followers. Jully is serving her purpose and has educated over 7,000 people.

I asked Jully about purpose and happiness.

"You have to know your core values," she said, "when purpose aligns with who you truly are, there's so much growth. It can lead to a purpose-driven business."

There truly is something meaningful when values, purpose, and work align.

"Your purpose will change because what makes you happy—your core values—can change over time," Jully added.

A parent's purpose can be their child. They are devoting time and energy to caring for someone other than themselves. As kids age, parents don't need to devote as much time and energy to their kids. Many parents have shared a need to find a new purpose. It's the same sentiment shared by retirees whose sense of purpose was work-related. After leaving their career, the search begins to find a purposeful replacement.

You'll grow and change as you gain new experiences. It's a good thing too. As time passes, you're adding more layers of what makes you ... you. The Happy Spirit is evolving and spiritually developing through your human journey.

There's another lesson I want you to know: serving a purpose can be profitable. The Happy Spirit serving its purpose often has big financial rewards. The alignment of spiritual and financial energy is powerful.

"But you must be mindful," says Jully. "You can get overwhelmed and burnt out serving purpose too."

I do caution you not to sacrifice other wellness dimensions. You might find yourself burning the midnight oil and choosing work over the family when serving a purpose. It will impact your happiness and well-being. You can experience spiritual stress too. Allow your mind, body, and spirit to rest.

BEING MINDFUL AND TIMELY

Time is finite, but time is conceptually infinite. Your spirit is separate but philosophically a part of something whole.

Mindfulness is awareness of the present moment—the gift of time.

Time connects us with others through shared experiences. The legacy we all leave behind is how we live and treat each other.

I don't think you'll ever be fully satisfied until you are spiritually filled. Invest in spiritual growth.

In Happy Spirit, we are mindful of our approach to living. There are many mindfulness practices available online and in books. I've developed my own practice to support a happy life. Mindfulness allows me to slow down, pause, and acknowledge the journey. It helps manage my stress and energizes my spirit. Studies show mindfulness is associated with a higher level of happiness, too.[4]

I refer to my core mindfulness practice as IAGA, an acronym for intention, affirmation, gratitude, and appreciation. It does include self-reflection and prayer too.

- **Intention** is what you hope to bring about. It's your determination to do a specific action. In the morning, I normally sit at the edge of my bed and think of my intentions for the day. It might be as simple as "I will do yoga" or "I will invest $100." Your intentions can set your mind for positive actions leading to results.

- **Affirmation** is a statement of action that something is true. Throughout the day, I'll spend a few minutes affirming the positive actions I'm taking. It can sound like "I am doing yoga" or "I am investing." Noticing the actions I'm taking makes me happy. And research has shown that affirmations activate specific parts of the brain associated with reward.[5]

- **Gratitude** is being thankful and appreciative of what has transpired. It recenters my thoughts on the positive results for what is. For instance, I'll say, "I am grateful for my yoga practice" or "I am grateful I can invest today." You can be grateful for anything, big or small. Studies have shown that "gratitude is strongly and consistently associated with greater happiness."[6]

- **Appreciation** is recognizing the people or things that contribute to well-being. We are rarely able to do things on our own. I will send emails, direct messages, and texts to family, friends, colleagues, and businesses. I want them to know my appreciation for their assistance in my journey in small and big ways. Acknowledge people in your life who've given support. Appreciation is similar to gratitude but requires you to take action. Allow for humility and connectivity. When you let people know how helpful they are, you spread positivity, and you'll experience positive mood changes, too.

My mindfulness practice includes self-reflection and prayer. I often reflect on past experiences for understanding, not judgment. This practice allows for more awareness of my thoughts, feelings, and actions. The insight often leads to positive changes in my behavior.

Prayer is another mindfulness tool. It's a reminder that I am connected to something greater, and I am never truly alone. Whatever your faith may be, it should support and connect you with others.

"Remember who you are connected to and who you have access to, through your faith, through your beliefs," Weslia shared.

You are connected to something greater. And you are truly never alone.

THE INSPIRED DIMENSIONS

Happy Spirit isn't about indoctrination into a religious belief or New Age spiritualism. It's about your connection to self as part of something greater. Some people attain so much material wealth, but their spiritual development is stunted. And there are people in this world with little materialistic wealth who find spiritual growth.

You can buy happiness by investing time in your spiritual development.

Spiritual health is needed for overall well-being. Your spiritual wellness helps you against insurmountable odds. You can tap into your spiritual reserves when you're mentally suffering or in physical pain. Believing there's a reason for the struggles, even though you don't understand them, can give you acceptance for what is. It's given me inner peace to acknowledge there's much I can't control in the world but to accept responsibility for what I can control—my mind, body, and spirit.

Without awareness of the Happy Spirit dimension, some people do harmful things for money that cause psychological issues, physical pain, social inequality, and environmental disasters.

When you're aligned with spirit, you have heightened awareness. It leads to different choices and a new path to a fulfilling and happier life. You give to others without sacrificing yourself. You realize a deeper connection transcending space and time. We are, after all, a human tribe hurtling through space. Our existence, some physicists say, is almost impossible, but here we are ... existing.

Whether you believe in a spirit or not, you've felt the void, wondered about purpose, and pondered the meaning of your existence.

How will you become inspired?

YOUR HAPPY TO-DO LIST

Practice mindfulness. Use the IAGA practice daily to help connect to yourself and with others. Journaling is another mindfulness tool that allows for self-reflection.

Find community. Engage with people who share your faith, challenge indoctrination, and strengthen your beliefs.

Give. Help others; volunteer for a cause; and share your knowledge, time, and skills.

Create. We are meant to create and add to the collective human experience. You may have noticed your positive feelings when you've created something. Look at your core values and see how you can help yourself and serve others through a creative effort.

HAPPY DIMENSION CONCLUSION

A good friend of mine has worked in hospice for over a decade. Through the years, Ralph and I chatted about people's reflections on their death bed. Many of the stories he's shared fall into these happy dimensions.

People rejoiced over experiences and memories with family and friends. They fondly talked about passion projects and meaningful work. Some did have regrets about not taking care of their bodies, taking too long to forgive others, or not spending enough time on the things that matter.

In the years he's worked, no one ever said they wished they had more money or worked more hours. Many didn't want more time either: they simply reflected on how they used their time. Some shared life advice: enjoy your youth, meet interesting people, follow more curiosities, and live *your* life.

Ralph shared that many people in hospice are often at peace. But he's shared stories of the living: family members visiting their loved one's final moments who can't help but talk about money, inheritance, and bills. And that's because money may not be everything, but it impacts most things, even at death. The lesson: it's essential to improve financial health to live happy lives and perhaps inspire our loved ones to do the same.

	What you've learned
Happy Life	You only live once; make it a happy life.
Happy Money	Living financially free.
Happy Work	Rewire; don't retire.
Happy Mind	Invest in yourself and learn continually.
Happy Heart	Memories appreciate; stuff depreciates.
Happy Body	Be kind to your body; it's priceless.
Happy Social	Connections are your lifeline.
Happy Space	Free your space and yourself.
Happy Spirit	Serve a purpose, not a purchase.

PRACTICAL APPROACH TO BUY HAPPINESS

When you're making a happiness purchase, ask yourself, "What's the wellness return?" Go through the dimensions to determine how they will affect your well-being.

Let's consider your taking a new job with a higher salary: that's good for your financial health. But what happens to other dimensions? Will the long commute or higher demand affect your psychological health? Will work travel impact your physical body? Will you work more and socialize less?

My aim for this book was to share the importance of the quality of your life, not just the quantity of years. You can choose happiness by focusing your resources—time and money—on wellness.

WHAT'S NEXT

You've just read through the happy dimensions. You've learned about the interconnectedness of the eight dimensions, how money affects them, and how to use your strengths to counterbalance areas that need support.

Think of the happy dimensions as batteries. You can tap into a dimension with full energy to help you with a depleted area. Take time to reenergize by resting and removing yourself from situations that drain your batteries. Lean into situations that fill them up.

You can use your financial batteries to support other dimensions. With money, you can find a better job, a safer neighborhood, and afford an experience to work on your mental and emotional health. You would own more of your time to devote to meaningful work, social interactions, and purpose. When you're financially healthy, you'll have more resources *to spend on wellness to buy happiness*.

Okay, it's time to get your money done right. We are going to shift gears from learning to doing. In Book III, you'll gain strategies to improve your financial health. With improved financial wellness, you'll have the Happy Money strengths to affect the happy dimensions positively.

A Spoken Word Poetic Break

The Acorn Within

There were times I believed I was a joke,
I was oh so ... broke.
Going through these stressful situations,
All I saw were my limitations.
I was having all these physical symptoms,
Without knowing the failure of my mental systems.
You see I needed to get out of my head,
The first step was to get out of bed.
Off I went out the door,
To go out and explore.
I found that during my walk out there
It became easier to think...in here..with care.
So I went further on this path, this trek,
And with the sun beating down my neck,
I took comfort in shade,
To contemplate the life choices I've made.
Sitting underneath this big oak tree,
on the ground, I found,
An oak nut, a little seed, an acorn, you see.

I pondered how something so small,
can grow into something so strong,
Could I've been wrong...
The leaps I want to make,
Starts with small steps I need to take.
Even though I felt small, I matter,
Causing my limiting beliefs to shatter.
Broke was a temporary instance,
Poor was a state of existence,
Often, I felt behind,
Because I hadn't shifted my mind.
Wealth is a state of being,
Aware of our mind, body, and soul,
Living, fully in our life's goal.
It's true,
Money impacts most things,
some things, a thing,
But money isn't,
everything.
Man,
wait, human,
create your plan.
Free yourself from debt and despair,
not solely on credit repair.
Grow your net worth,
believe in your self-worth.
Allow money to flow,
not through a spreadsheet of deprivation,
or drawn-out deliberation.
Flow with intention,
Because life is best lived,
with purposeful direction.
Ding...do you hear that chime,
my time is coming to a close,
so let me end,
with a little more lyrical prose.

Time is not money.
Money is printed.
Time is limited.
Time is the most valuable resource you possess,
become obsess.
Be willing to save and spend that dime,
And learn to value your time.
Because life isn't,
about sacrifice and sadness.
Life is sacrifice,
in choosing happiness.
Underneath that big oak tree,
I found the little acorn,
within me.
I realized my life,
was no small joke,
and at that moment,
I woke.
*Watch the spoken word poem: www.jasonvitug.com/acorn

A HAPPY EXERCISE

Think about your money and life situation. How can you express yourself creatively? Can it be in prose, poetry, music, video, dance, painting, drawing, knitting, or performance art?

I wrote my first spoken word, *The Acorn Within*, in the fall of 2019. I didn't share the poetic prose until September 2020. I was afraid of criticism of the rhyming, structure, and performance. Creating it, however, gave me satisfaction, and sharing it with others made me happy.

BOOK III

Choosing Financial Happiness

Wealth consists not in having great possessions, but in having few wants.

—Epictetus

What is the purpose of money if not to help you become happy?

If you're not using money to reduce stress, buy back time, and become happier, you're doing it all wrong. Yes, wrong. I'm the first to admit I used money to buy the wrong things. I didn't know any better back then, but now I do.

We've come full circle: we're back to where it all started in the happy dimensions section.

Happy Money is financial wellness.

Financial wellness is a holistic state of living through the *active pursuit* of financial knowledge, planning, and goal setting to live a happy life. When you have a good grasp of personal financial knowledge, you can make better decisions to achieve goals that support well-being.

Knowledge is power: *financial knowledge is life-changing*.

Research conducted by the Institute for Social and Economic Research revealed that "high financial capability is associated with higher levels of psychological health."[1] So, you'll experience less financial stress. And another study indicated that individuals with higher financial literacy are happier.[2]

Continue to follow your financial curiosity.

You don't have to know everything all at once. Becoming financially literate is an ongoing process. You'll face new money situations as you progress in life. It's vital to know there is a solution to every financial situation.

There is a lot to personal finance. My aim isn't to tell you about everything. My plan is to guide you to financial freedom.

Let's get you into the Happy Money zone.

CHOOSING FINANCIAL HAPPINESS

In the Happy Money zone, you'll gain insights and learn how to improve your financial health. I will zoom out to give you a broad context of money, then zoom in to the finer details with strategies and specific tactics. This process is called the Smile Money Steps.

As you've learned in previous chapters, happiness is about having choices and options. Healthy finances will give you more options and help you make better choices. Taking this money journey is a momentous step in choosing happiness. It may be challenging at times, but it will be life-changing. I'll walk you through three parts.

First, you'll learn to shift your **money beliefs** to improve your financial behaviors and habits.

Second, you'll calculate your **money vitals** to assess your financial health.

Third, you'll start the **money journey** to financial freedom.

Are you ready to make your Happy Money, smile?

Nine Uplifting Signs of Financial Happiness

Before proceeding to the first step, let's determine how you're doing with the money. Here are signs of financial happiness.

1. **You don't lose sleep over money.** If you can sleep at night without worrying about your job, bills, and the economy, you're financially stable even if you haven't hit all your money goals. This isn't to say that you don't have anxieties. But, unlike some people, your worries aren't solely money-related.

Happy Tip

Have a coping technique to deal with stressful situations, such as taking a walk or breathwork.

2. **You can pay your bills.** Knowing you can pay your bills is a good sign. No one likes the rising cost of living, from rent to food to entertainment. Everything is getting more expensive. But if you take a step back, you might realize your lifestyle is affordable.

Happy Tip

Lower your cash outflows. Do a quarterly audit of your expenses to reduce unnecessary bills like unused subscriptions.

3. **You never overdraw your accounts.** Never having to use overdraft protection means you have adequate cash flow into your bank account to cover bills, expenses, and debit card transactions. You also monitor your balances not to overspend.

Happy Tip

Set alerts with your accounts to get daily balances and transaction notifications.

4. **You use credit intentionally.** Using a credit card responsibly ensures you don't create long-term debt. Financially stable people don't use credit out of necessity or as an extension of their incomes. Credit is a choice that earns reward points and cashback on purchases.

Happy Tip

Don't charge anything on credit cards that you can't pay off in full within the grace period. Avoid paying interest charges and late fees.

5. **You are contributing to retirement plans.** The future is bright, and you plan to make it well into retirement. You contribute to your company's 401(k) or similar plan and may even have a Roth IRA.

Happy Tip

Contribute the amount to get the full employer match in a 401(k) plan.

6. **You're paying yourself first.** Financial happiness isn't only about paying bills and having minimum debt, it also involves having the disposable income to take care of financial needs when they arise. This means you have a savings strategy in place.

Happy Tip

Set it and forget. Use automatic transfers into a savings account each payday.

7. **You are living within your means.** You don't need to earn a lot to be financially stable. You spend less than you earn and make savings a priority. And some of your savings are invested for independence.

Happy Tip

Aim to save 20% of your pre-tax income through a combination of retirement contributions, automatic savings transfers, and general investing.

8. **You have a backup plan.** Maintain your happiness with a backup plan, such as a cash reserve for emergencies and unforeseen expenses or a side hustle to supplement your income.

Happy Tip

Have an emergency savings plan that includes a rainy day fund with $1,000.

9. **You get asked for money advice.** Your close friends and relatives may observe your money habits and respect your wise decisions. They might feel you are the best person to get financial advice from.

Happy Tip

Be mindful of the advice you share with family or friends. You don't want to strain any relationship or stress yourself. Recommend your favorite money books or give them a copy of this book. Share helpful blogs, YouTube channels, and podcasts. And if you're working with professionals like financial planners, make an introduction.

Rest assured if you've discovered you need specific help not covered in the book. There are a ton of resources available on phroogal.com/smilemoney.

CHAPTER **13**

Part 1: Money Beliefs: Your Thoughts and Feelings

I t starts with money beliefs that inform your financial habits and behaviors. These beliefs either cause distress or lead to success. The standard money mindset definition is the thoughts (Happy Mind) and feelings (Happy Heart) you have developed about money based on your life experiences.

It's what drives your decisions about spending, savings, and investing. Having a growth mindset can help improve your financial life. On the other hand, a fixed mindset can hinder your ability to achieve financial success.

A growth mindset is essential to financial health and creating wealth. Some examples include:

- Having money goals is vital to me.
- Credit is used for leverage.

- I contribute to retirement accounts.
- Investing is for me.

A *fixed mindset* can often lead to self-sabotaging financial behaviors. Some examples include:

- I will never make enough money to realize my dreams.
- Debt is a part of life.
- I don't have enough money to save.
- Investing is only for the rich.

Take time to reflect on your thoughts and feelings.
What type of beliefs do you hold?
Make an effort to know how you feel when money comes up. Do you cringe when someone mentions money? Do you tune out when others talk about investments? How do you feel about debt?

TELL ME WHAT YOU WANT

In personal finance, there's an emphasis on knowing the differences between needs and wants. The curious thing about our minds is how often they blur the line between needs and wants. It causes many of us to buy needless things, blow up our budget, and create financial stress.

I'll remind you: needs are expenses that are required and essential such as shelter, food, medicine, and clothing; wants aren't necessary but desired, like a new smartphone, luxury car, or pair of sneakers. The significant difference between needs and wants is simple.

- Needs are things you have to have.
- Wants are things you would like to have.

THIS IS WHAT YOU REALLY WANT

This may not come as a surprise. It's easy to choose between needing food to eat versus wanting the latest smartphone. It gets a bit more challenging to determine: what you want and what you really want. What we say we want is not what we *really* want.

- We need a car and want a luxury vehicle, but what we *really* want is to make the drive to a miserable job more enjoyable.
- We need a vacation and want an all-inclusive island getaway, but what we *really* want is to get away from the rat race.
- We need a place to live and want to own a house, but what we *really* want is the safety and comforts of a home.
- We need sneakers and want the $300 fashionable Nikes, but what we *really* want is social acceptance.

How you think (mental health) and feel (emotional health) influences what you want. And the reason you can't get what you *really* want has less to do with money and more with your well-being.

Hopefully, you realize your real wants are less about materialism and more about happiness. Without spending mindfully, however, you can mistake purchasing "what you say you want," which makes "what you really want" all the more challenging to own.

To help you become a mindful spender, I recommend using three questions when making a purchase, big or small.

1. Ask yourself, *"Do I need it?"*
2. Ask yourself again, *"Do I need it now?"*
3. Then ask yourself, *"What will happen if I don't have it?"*

To help you become a happy spender, ask two additional questions.

4. Take a deep breath and ask yourself, *"What am I feeling right now?"*
5. Then take another deep breath and ask yourself, *"Is there anything else I'd rather do?"*

The immediate benefit of asking these questions is to delay the purchase. It gives your mind a momentary pause that might be enough to keep you from spending. Ultimately, buying "what you need" and "what you want" is up to you.

What do you really want out of life?

Here's what I think you really want.

You Really Want to Create

It's okay to want money. There's no shame in wanting it because the reality is such we need money to live in this world.

Money isn't the end goal; money is the tool to achieve the goals.

You've learned money is a tool that can solve problems.

What are your money problems?

If you're struggling to pay for rent or afford groceries, your brain will focus on meeting those basic needs first. Sure, you'll think about the macroeconomic forces affecting housing and food prices, but chances are you'll find yourself mentally exhausted. And if you don't have the money to feed yourself properly, you'll affect your physical health too. Once you have money to solve money problems, it's easier to create solutions for life problems.

In Book I, I asked you to finish the statement: Money is _____. Let's go with: *money is a tool.*

Now, I want you to complete this statement: Money is a tool to create _____ (fill in the blank).

There are no right or wrong answers. Whatever words are used to fill in the blank is what's most important to you right now. Thinking back on how money can buy *wellness things*, your statements can be like this:

- Money is a tool to create *stability at home.*
- Money is a tool to create *memories.*
- Money is a tool to create *my business.*
- Money is a tool to create *jobs for my community.*
- Money is a tool to create *social change.*
- Money is a tool to create *equality and equity.*
- Money is a tool to create *peace of mind.*
- Money is a tool to create *happiness.*

The wonderful thing about this exercise is how it directs you to a sense of purpose (Happy Spirit). It gives us meaning, connection, and direction, supporting our happiness and well-being.

So what do you want to create?

You Really Want Wealth

Building wealth isn't a selfish act. Wealth inspires confidence, fosters security, and supports peace of mind. As a wealthy person, you will be good for the world. I want you to be wealthy!

Take the time to ponder these questions.

What's your mindset about wealth? What does wealth mean to you? Do you feel wealthy?

Wealth can mean many things to different people. Some may view wealth in terms of income while others in meaningful connections (Happy Social). There's also a macroeconomic definition for wealth measured solely in money with benchmarks that vary greatly from one nation to another. You might be surprised to know that living in America puts all of us, generally speaking, in the top 1% of the wealth in the world. "As Americans, we underestimate how rich we are compared to the rest of the world." The average person in the world earns $2,100 annually.[1] We are a rich nation, but are we truly wealthy? I'll leave you to research global wealth.

Now, in its most basic definition, *wealth* is the abundance of cash and other financial investments or physical and digital assets that are convertible to cash. Since defining wealth can be as subjective as answering, "What does happiness mean to you?" I'll focus on discussing wealth as it pertains to finances.

Wealthy and rich are not the same thing

To some, the words *rich* and *wealthy* mean the same thing, but I want you to understand there's a difference. Rich is what you see, and wealth is what you feel. Most people who look rich aren't wealthy, but wealthy people are rich. A rich person has income to spend, but a wealthy person has money that grows. Wealth lessens the financial stress you'll experience.

Wealth is a state of being your-self, and rich is a state of being your-stuff.

Generally, when we think of being rich, we associate it with a lavish lifestyle and the ability to spend freely. From the outside, a rich person might live in a beautiful house and drive a luxury car. We might even envy them, but we don't know the cost of their lifestyle.

Let's imagine a rich person who makes $250,000 a year. "Wow, they are rich," you say based purely on their income. However, looking deeper, you might discover that a large mortgage, a high-interest car loan, and lifestyle expenses are more than their annual income. They are living well above their means. You might think this impossible, but a recent Lending Club survey found that 36% of people earning $250,000 or more are living paycheck to paycheck.[2]

The opposite is true for wealthy people.

I've learned many wealthy people live a life we can relate to: they have modest homes, drive used cars, and are still working. However, a wealthy person prioritizes buying assets that appreciate and assets that generate income, such as real estate, business ventures, or stock investments. The wealthy grow money for security and peace of mind, not social status.

Wealthy mindset	Rich mindset
- Builds long-term wealth	- Earns a lot of money
- Sees saving and investing as a priority	- Sees spending as a priority
- Buys appreciating assets	- Buys depreciating assets
- Holds income-producing assets	- Focuses on spending goals
- Carries little to no consumer debt	- Believes credit can pay for lifestyle
- Lives below their means	- Lives above their means
- Spends to live well	- Spends to show a lifestyle
- Believes money buys back time	- Exchanges more time for money

Wealth is measured by assets, not possessions.

Financial wealth is measured by what you have of monetary value. It is the total value of your home equity, savings accounts, investment portfolio, art collection, or stash of gold in a safe deposit box. Sure, you may own clothing and tech gadgets that you can sell for cash, but these items depreciate in value. And if you think some of your possessions are collector items, it means you have a plan for future liquidation.

Wealth is saved, not spent.

I once believed wealth meant having the ability to spend freely. The more money I made, the more I could spend. I lived way above my means. It trapped me into living paycheck to paycheck. I wasn't building wealth because I wasn't buying appreciating assets. Fortunately, I learned to make money with money.

You can make $100,000 a year and spend all of it, or you can make $85,000 a year, save and invest some of it, and have a net worth of $25,000.

Let's use the example of Keira and Adriana.

Keira makes $100,000 a year and lives a "pretty good" life. She believes her income will continue rising and plans to work until retirement. She does manage to save a little through her company's 401(k) plan. On the other hand, Adriana makes $85,000 a year and lives below her means. She saves $25,000 a year through a combination of 401(k) contributions and automatic transfers to her savings goals. Adriana wants to retire early.

Who do you think is creating wealth?

	Annual income	Annual expenses	Saved and invested	Net worth *(after 2 years)*
Keira Living to keep up appearances	$100,000	$96,000	$4,000	$8,000
Adriana Living to reach financial independence	$85,000	$60,000	$25,000	$50,000

Wealth is net worth, not income.

Adriana is a 26-year-old analyst who makes $85,000 a year. She has a net worth of $50,000 from a combination of 401(k) contributions, general investing, and a savings account. Compared to Keira, she's way ahead of the game and on track to achieve her retirement goals.

Net worth is the most accurate measure of your wealth and is the best indicator of financial health at a given time. Your net worth is the difference between what you own (assets) and what you owe (liabilities).

- Assets are things of value that can be converted into cash, such as savings accounts, real estate, investment accounts, and other personal property (cars, computers, collectibles).

▪ Liabilities are your debt obligations such as auto loans, credit cards, mortgages, student loans, medical bills, and any other installment payment you're making.

Take me as an example. I used to believe wealth only meant having a high income. I focused on climbing the corporate ladder to increase my salary. However, as my income increased, I experienced lifestyle inflation—an increase in spending as the income went up. I may have looked rich to family and friends, but my net worth remained low.

Many wealthy people understand a little-known truth. The first step to wealth is through earned income—money from a paycheck. But, the size of your paycheck does not determine if you'll grow your net worth. Continue spending your entire income, and you'll never build wealth. Choose instead to live below your income by investing a percentage of your salary: contribute to your employer's retirement plan, invest in the stock market, and buy appreciating and income-generating assets.

In short, the key to wealth is your net worth. To be wealthy, you'll need to have a positive net worth. Tracking your net worth helps monitor your financial activities. You can see the impact of increasing income, growing savings, investing, and buying assets. When you're creating wealth, you build a future with more ownership over your time.

What's your net worth?

You Really Want More Time

Time is a finite resource. You might have heard the saying "time is money," but that is only half true. On one side of the coin, time is an asset. On the other side, it's a liability. Time is the asset we are born with and taught to exchange for money. Doing so allows us to buy our needs and wants. But, time is also a liability that we are born into with a due date. Time, as a liability, must be repaid and we can do so with a life well lived.

How can you live well?

It boils down to holding the metaphorical time coin. Shifting your beliefs that time is just money. It's you realizing the value of time and how to spend it best.

Unfortunately, for many, the time asset is owned by someone else. We are exchanging our time for a paycheck. Some are often overworked and underpaid. This time-at-work-for-pay cycle is exhausting and doesn't leave much room for joy and happiness. It takes you away from what you *really* want to do, such as spending *happy time* with family and friends and hobbies and projects.

EXCHANGING YOUR TIME FOR A PAYCHECK

Let's look at our friends, Keira and Adriana.

We can determine the monetary value of time through income. If you're a salaried employee, you probably don't think of hours as money. Income doesn't change based on the number of hours worked. So you may not think about how that is impacting your money.

	Annual salary	Weekly income	Hours worked	Hourly wage
Keira	$100,000	$1,923	60	$32.05
Adriana	$85,000	$1,634	40	$40.85

In this example, you'll notice Adriana, with a lower annual salary, makes more per hour compared to Keira. Perhaps, Keira working 60 hours a week is why she's burnt out and spends her entire paycheck to feel better. Let's persuade Keira to work fewer hours and make more while regaining her time.

	Annual salary	Weekly income	Hours worked	Hourly wage
Keira	$100,000	$1,923	40	$48.07

Reducing her working hours, Keira learned she could give herself a raise of $16 per hour. What can Keira do? She can discuss a better work-life balance with her manager or perhaps ask for a raise.

If neither of those things happens, Keira may need to find a more suitable job that values her time and experience.

You don't need to calculate your hourly wage if you're an hourly employee.

The amount you're paid per hour doesn't fluctuate based on the number of hours worked. You can only make more money by working more hours (e.g., exchanging your time). The goal then is to make more during the hours you work, too. You can also consider gaining new skills and education to find a salaried job.

Apply this scenario to your work life.

How can you work less and make more money?

SPENDING YOUR TIME ON STUFF

You've exchanged a lot of time at work for money. Others might see the results because you own expensive and luxurious goods. These purchases may temporarily make you happy, but you want to feel sustainably happier.

When you understand the value of time, you no longer buy stuff to show off to others. You *show up* for family and friends because you own your time.

Have you ever thought of your purchases in terms of time?

Doing so is an eye-opening exercise. It can be alarming but helpful. It can lead to shifting your money beliefs. Consider the scenario of buying the latest iPad for $799. It's a shiny new tech toy. You imagine how much better your life would be. The thought of owning the iPad makes you happy.

Let's take a look at this purchase based on income and time.

	Item	Price	Hourly wage	Happy time
Keira	iPad	$799	$32.05	25 hours
Adriana	iPad	$799	$40.85	19.5 hours
Hourly employee	iPad	$799	$15.00	53 hours

In this example, buying the iPad will cost anywhere from 19.5 to 53 hours of happy time. Thinking about purchases through time gives it a different perspective. Adriana and Keira must work around half a week to afford it. For the hourly employee, the iPad means working for almost 1.5 weeks.

Is it worth it?

By looking at this example, you can state people need to be paid more: I wouldn't argue with you. The point still stands as the results will be similar. You can substitute the hourly wage with any amount and see how a purchase reduces happy time.

Take a look at a recent item you've purchased.

How much happy time did it cost you?

I am not here to tell you what to buy. Or scold you for spending money. It is your money. You can spend money on stuff or use it to reclaim time. As you read in Book I, ownership over time is a crucial ingredient of happiness. And if I haven't emphasized enough, I want you to be happy.

What life do you want to create? You don't want more stuff. What you *really* want is money to create the life of your dreams, wealth that allows you to be your true self, and the time to spend on people and projects that matter to you.

Now that you've shifted your money beliefs, it's time to assess your financial health.

CHAPTER 14

Part 2:
Money Vitals:
Your Financial
Health Numbers

You cannot achieve financial freedom if you don't know how you're starting the journey. By calculating your money vitals, you determine areas of strength and uncover opportunities for improvement. The following financial numbers are the most essential.

1. Net worth (*security*).
2. Cash flow (*safety*).
3. Income number (*scalability*).
4. Credit score (*credibility*).
5. Debt-to-income (*movability*).

These five money vitals represent your financial health. Monitoring and improving these vitals support your well-being.

NET WORTH

It's the most crucial money vital and the best indicator of financial wealth. Net worth is your security number and tracks your asset-building progress. Some view financial health based on higher incomes, but wealth may remain flat even after income grows. Having debt can be worrisome, but when set against your assets, debt is used as leverage and placed into the proper financial perspective.

What you own minus what you owe.

Your net worth is the value of assets that remain after subtracting your liabilities.

If you have $100,000 in total assets and owe $75,000 in total liabilities, your net worth is $25,000. You would have a positive net worth, meaning your assets exceed your liabilities. It's an indication of good financial health. In contrast, having negative net worth increases the likelihood of future financial stress.

What is your net worth?

 Take Action

Calculate Your Net Worth Number

1. List your assets (what you own), estimate the value of each, and add up the total. These may include money in savings accounts, investments, the value of your car, the market value of a home, retirement accounts, etc.
2. List your liabilities (what you owe) and add up the total. These may include your loans, credit card balances, mortgage, etc.
3. Subtract what you own from what you owe.

Net worth = Assets (what you own)

−Liabilities (what you owe)

How Do You Compare?

Please understand the data shared below is for references only. Don't misconstrue the household's average and median net worth as targets for your situation.

The key to financial well-being is a personalized plan taking your lifestyle choices and retirement goals to set your net worth target.

The Typical Net Worth of Americans by Age

According to the most recent Federal Reserve data, the average net worth of American households is as follows:

Age	Average net worth	Median net worth
Under 35	$76,300	$13,900
35 to 44	$436,200	$91,300
45 to 54	$833,200	$168,600
55 to 64	$1,175,900	$212,500
65 to 74	$1,217,700	$266,400
75 or older	$997,600	$254,800

Source: Data from https://www.federalreserve.gov/publications/files/scf17.pdf.
Note: The average net worth takes the average of all data, including outliers that can skew the average. The median net worth gives you an idea of the middle point where half the data is more and the other half less. For example, if you're 30 years old with a net worth of $25,000, you may be below average, but you're in the top 50% of your age group.

CASH FLOW

The cash flow is your safety number indicating if your monthly income is sufficient to cover your monthly expenses. It indicates how safely you're spending your income. With positive cash flow, rest assured knowing you can afford your monthly expenses and have money to put towards other goals. In contrast, having a negative cash flow means cutting expenses and increasing income.

Cash flow is calculated monthly and can help determine if you live within, below, or above your means. Your cash flow includes the following:

- **Income**—salary, bonuses, hourly wages, self-employed, passive, or investment sources.

- **Fixed expenses**—essential costs and living expenses such as rent, mortgage, and utilities; groceries; and other monthly bills like debt payments.
- **Discretionary expenses**—non essential costs you can live without, such as streaming services or dining out.

If your monthly income is $5,000 and your monthly expenses are $4,000, you have a positive cash flow of $1,000. Because you're living below your means, you can allocate money towards savings and investment goals.

What is your cash flow?

 Take Action

Calculate Your Cash Flow

1. Add your monthly income from all sources (*after taxes and deductions*).
2. Add all monthly expenses (*rent/mortgage, utilities, subscriptions, loan payments, etc.*).
3. Subtract total monthly net income with the total monthly expenses.

Net cash flow = Total monthly net income
– Total monthly expenses

INCOME NUMBER

The income number is your scalability number, which signifies opportunities to build wealth. It helps you understand how money flows into your life. And supports financial security by identifying opportunities to diversify and multiply income sources to be less reliant on a single income.

Your income is the money made through wages at work, side hustles, and investment returns. We often focus only on the income from salaries, but it's important to know other ways to make money.

What's your income number?

 Take Action

Calculate Your Annual Income Number

1. Use your journal or a spreadsheet app.
2. In one column, list all your income sources from a primary job, part-time work, side gigs, dividends, etc.
3. Write the income made from each source in the second column.
4. Total the number of sources of income and amount of income.

CREDIT SCORE

The credit score is your credibility number indicating how lenders perceive you as a borrower. The credibility can lead to approvals for mortgages and other loans to help build wealth through leverage. It helps you shop for better financing and lowers the cost of borrowing.

A credit score is a number that measures your creditworthiness within the 300 to 850 range. Your score represents various information found in your credit report.

You want a good to excellent credit rating, but credit scores are not a signifier of wealth. A person with an excellent 800 credit score with a negative net worth is financially unhealthy.

What's your credit score?

Take Action

Get Your Free Credit Scores

1. Ask your bank or credit union about free credit scores.
2. Ask your existing credit card company about free credit scores.
3. For a current list of free credit score apps, visit phroogal.com/smilemoney.

As a general guideline, compare your score with these ranges.

- Excellent credit: 750+
- Good credit: 700–749
- Fair credit: 650–699
- Poor credit: 600–649
- Bad credit: below 600

DEBT-TO-INCOME

The debt-to-income ratio is your movability number determining if you can freely move. This money vital helps you understand your relationship with debt. Debt is a ball and chain, and can deny you the opportunity to move up in life. For example, leaving a bad job is much harder if you have debt.

Your debt-to-income (DTI) can show if you're over-leveraged, which means your income is allocated heavily for loan payments. Lenders also use the DTI ratio to determine if you can afford to take on another monthly payment. It also helps you decide if a loan is in your best interest and won't hurt your cash flow.

A higher DTI can mean the inability to cover debt or loan obligations in the future. You want to keep an eye on growing loan payments and stagnant income growth. A lower DTI indicates less risk to lenders, increasing approval odds for buying a home, refinancing mortgages, and consolidating credit card and student loan debt. Refinancing and consolidating debt could result in a positive net change in cash flow and net worth.

What's your DTI ratio?

Take Action

Calculate Your Debt-to-Income Ratio

1. Add your monthly bills (mortgage payments; student, auto, or other fixed monthly payments; credit card minimum monthly payments; other debts).
2. Divide the total of your monthly loan payments by your monthly gross income (income before taxes).
3. The result is a percentage called your debt-to-income ratio.

DTI Ratio = Total monthly debt payments/
Total gross monthly income

Example : Debt-to-income ratio

Step 1: Total monthly debt payments = $3,000
Step 2: Total gross income = $6,000
DTI Ratio = 0.50 = $3,000/$6,000
You can convert the decimal value into a percentage.
DTI Percentage = 50% = (0.50 × 100)
This makes it simpler to say that 50% of your gross income repays monthly debt obligations.

Congrats, you've just learned which numbers are vital to financial health. These money vitals can help you focus your efforts for better results.

Calculating your money vitals is about assessing where you are today so that you can chart a path to where you want to be in the future. It's important to know your starting point. It will help you determine if you've made progress without falling into the trap of comparing yourself to other people's journeys.

In the next chapter, you'll start your money journey and learn about strategies to improve these numbers.

CHAPTER 15

Part 3: Money Journey: Your Path to Financial Happiness

I t does not matter where you start, just as long as you've started the journey.

Before you begin the money journey, I want to remind you that happiness isn't the destination; you experience happiness along the way. In keeping with the happy dimensions, you don't want to sacrifice parts of your health for financial gain. I created the paths to guide you through the Happy Money zone.

SMILE MONEY STEPS

The Smile Money Paths simplifies important aspects of financial wellness into nine easy-to-follow paths. You can follow the paths sequentially, but they are designed to work independently. It works similarly to the happy dimensions: the paths are multilayered, overlap, and interconnect.

Working on one area will have an effect on another financial area. For instance, if your most pressing need is to eliminate debt, you can start with path 3, which often leads to better cash flow to fund savings and investment. Is the lack of money the main culprit? Start with path 4: earning more money could help you start investing. Are you financially healthy? Consider jumping ahead to path 9 to reach financial independence. You get the idea: it's customizable to you.

With that said, I've been intentional about how these paths are sequenced: read through them all. Then go back to any area where you especially need help.

As a Happy Money reminder, my goal is for you to experience less stress and improve your well-being. The money journey will help you own your time to grow your mind, feel your emotions, improve your body, and lift your spirits. You will gain more choices to pursue meaningful work, find healthy relationships, and inhabit Happy Spaces.

I wish I could include everything in this book, but it would turn into a textbook. Each path is a short chapter. I've only highlighted key areas that are essential to making your money smile. Here are the Smile Money Paths:

- Path 1: Save for the unexpected.
- Path 2: You're going to retire one day.
- Path 3: Debt is holding you back.
- Path 4: You need to make more money.
- Path 5: Start investing right now.
- Path 6: Be creditworthy, not credit hungry.
- Path 7: For your protection, please.
- Path 8: Your ultimate safety net.
- Path 9: Independence is your birthright.

For more resources for each specific step, visit phroogal.com/smilemoney.

CHAPTER 16

Path 1: Save for the Unexpected

E mergencies happen: it's not a matter of if but a matter of when.

What happens if you have an emergency expense? Perhaps, your dog swallowed a toy, and the vet charges $2,000 to operate. Do you have the money? Or maybe, your car needs new brakes that will cost $500. Can you cover the expense? What will you do if you become unemployed?

Save for rainy days and opportunities.

Feel secure knowing you can cover unexpected expenses and periods of job loss. You'll benefit from an emergency savings plan. It's a critical element of personal finance because it acts as an insurance policy for your earnings.

An emergency fund strategy can give you security and peace of mind. It includes two types of savings accounts for small and big emergencies.

The rainy day fund.

It pays for minor inconveniences like a flat tire or an unexpected medical bill. Have at least $1,000 in a rainy day fund, or use your auto insurance deductible as a target amount. I had a friend who was involved in a car accident and could not pick up his car for three weeks. He didn't have the money for the deductible. My friend's financial stress ballooned: his insurance carrier billed him for the car rental days passed the available pickup date.

The opportunity fund.

The fund cover periods of unemployment, reduced work hours, or incapacitation. It's called an opportunity fund because of the time you get back. It's a positive spin on an otherwise negative situation. Since you're not spending time at work, you can search for a new job with less stress. I want you to save six months of your monthly basic living expenses: the bare-bones budget that covers housing, food, and necessities. Decide what necessities are needed so you don't feel stifled. Remember that a more expensive lifestyle will require more money to be saved.

A few things to remember about the emergency savings plan:

- After using the money in either fund, replenish it as soon as possible.
- Use auto-transfers each payday to keep you on track to meet the savings targets.
- Decide whether having the accounts at your primary bank is wise: some feel tempted to spend the money.
- An alternative is using a high-yield savings account (HYSA) offered by an online bank or credit union. You can easily find the best savings rates online or by visiting phroogal.com.
- To further help, I suggest customizing the title of the savings accounts. Many financial institutions offer you the option of changing the generic "savings account" name to "$1,000 for those rainy days."

Last, emergency savings aren't going to prevent a disaster, but having money helps make a disaster less devastating. At the minimum, your savings reduces or eliminates the financial stress of the emergency, giving you the mental bandwidth to deal with the associated life issue. These funds help you refocus on what matters and get you back on track to wellness.

	Goal	Amount needed	Monthly contribution
Rainy Day Fund	$1,000		
Opportunity fund	Six months of basic living expenses		

 Take Action

1. Open your rainy day fund.
2. Open your opportunity fund.
3. Make an initial deposit and set up automatic transfers each payday.

CHAPTER 17

Path 2: You're Going to Retire One Day

Retirement is a financial number, not simply an age.

We will all retire one day, whether by choice, age, or ailment. For a happy life, make it a choice.

People define *retirement* differently: some picture themselves sitting on a beach, while others want to continue to work. And many more might think of retirement as a time for hobbies and passion projects. You might think of retirement as having more time with family and friends. However you choose to define *retirement*, you must financially plan for it.

Retirement planning is fundamental in creating a secure financial future and a lower-stress lifestyle. And starting as early as possible lets you choose when to retire instead of waiting for the retirement age set by a government agency. Whether you desire to retire early or work until full retirement age, you'll need to manage your money to set up a comfortable retirement.

How much do you need to save for retirement?

Well, that depends. Many financial advisors use a $1 million target as a retirement goal. But the amount of money you need to retire well (however you define it) is a matter of your lifestyle. The lower the cost of your lifestyle, the smaller the amount of money you need.

"You should know the actual lifestyle you want to live," Kevin states, "you'll have better luck in reaching your retirement goals that way."

Kevin Matthews II is the founder of buildingbread.com. He is a former financial advisor who managed a $140 million portfolio. As an investment educator, he encourages people to start investing sooner and think long term. When it comes to retirement goals, Kevin shared that there are good benchmarks to compare yourself to but that you should not get caught up in them. You should plan your retirement goals based on your happy lifestyle.

And that's what I've learned with benchmarks. They are good to see how we're doing but can also add tremendous stress. When you see you're far behind, it's demotivating and does the opposite of what is intended. I follow a simpler and personalized approach. Consider the following two-step approach:

- Step 1: Calculate your retirement needs.
- Step 2: Know your retirement investment options.

STEP 1: CALCULATE YOUR RETIREMENT NEEDS

Envision your retirement. Consider how much that lifestyle will cost. Perhaps, your lifestyle will remain the same, but chances are good your expenses will go down: mortgages, student loans, and childcare might no longer exist.

Use the rule of 25.

Take your projected annual expense and multiply by 25 to get your target retirement goal. The equation: Retirement Goal = Annual Lifestyle Expense × 25.

If your retirement goal seems inflated because of your current lifestyle, the great news is that you have control over lessening your expenses.

Be mindful of lifestyle inflation.

It creates a dual stress scenario: it inflates the amount of money needed for retirement and leads to never having extra money to invest.

Contribute to your retirement right now.

Your age and when you plan to retire impact the amount of money needed to save and invest. "Ten years from now, you'd wish you started today, so just start," Kevin said. "However, if you start later, it simply means you'll need to either contribute more or postpone retirement. It is about utilizing time to grow your money."

There's a dual benefit to starting sooner: (1) you give money more time to grow by taking advantage of compounding—when interest earned starts earning interest too, and (2) you'll need less money to reach your retirement goal. Investing sooner will be to your benefit when it comes to retiring happily.

HOW MUCH DO YOU NEED IN RETIREMENT?

The rule of 25 is a helpful way to determine your target retirement needs. For example, if your retirement lifestyle expenses will be $50,000 annually, you can multiply that by 25.

Retirement Goal = Annual Lifestyle Expense × 25

Projected annual lifestyle expense	Multiply by 25	Retirement goal
$50,000	x 25	$1,250,000

How Much Do You Need to Reach Your Retirement Goal?

Example: If you are 20 years old, starting with $1,000 and contributing $500 per month, it will take you 40 years to reach $1.25 million. This assumes an expected rate of return of 7%.

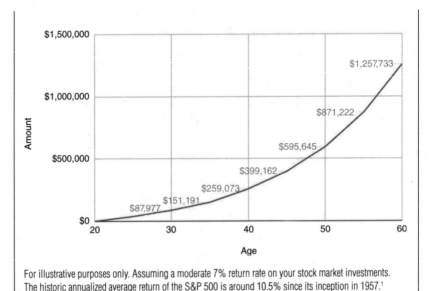

For illustrative purposes only. Assuming a moderate 7% return rate on your stock market investments. The historic annualized average return of the S&P 500 is around 10.5% since its inception in 1957.[1]

STEP 2: KNOW YOUR RETIREMENT INVESTMENT OPTIONS

Courtney Richardson, an attorney and financial expert behind the Ivy Investor, shared, "Most retirement planning involves employer 401(k) plans, pensions, and IRAs." Your tax-advantaged account options include 401(k)s and IRAs, giving you tax breaks and reduced tax liabilities.

1. Contribute to your employer's 401(k) plan or similar retirement plan.

With 401(k)s, you can contribute pretax income into target-date funds that might include an employer match. Pre-tax retirement accounts let you deduct your contributions from taxes in the year you make them.

Courtney recommends getting to know your employer plans, participating, and maxing out contributions. "Most people don't opt-in and lose the money of the employer match," Courtney said.

You are tasked with enrolling in the 401(k) plan, setting your contribution percentage, and ensuring you're at least contributing to the employer match. Kevin and Courtney shared the sentiment, "don't leave money on the table."

2. Investing using a Roth IRA for after-tax contributions.

Roth IRAs let you contribute money that you've paid taxes on already. They are a good way to invest for retirement. "They grow tax-free, and the contributions can be withdrawn without penalty," Courtney said.

The downsides are the annual contribution limit, but until you retire, you could save a lot of money. So, in the end, it can pay off. The IRS determines the contribution maximums and income limits. Visit the irs.gov website to determine what they are for the tax year.

Are you feeling anxious about retirement?

Take a long and deep inhale. Followed by a slow exhale. Take a look at your current retirement savings: you might already be on track to achieve the goal by the time you're in your sixties.

HOW MUCH WILL YOUR RETIREMENT GROW?

Sophia began investing at 20 years old and contributes $10,000 annually through her 401(k) plan. At the age of 60, she has $2,285,840. Her total contributions are $410,000.

Greta began investing at 30 years old and contributes $10,000 annually through her 401(k) plan. At age 60, she has $1,086,852. Her total contributions are $310,000.

Sophia's retirement account is $1,198,988 more than Greta with just an additional $100,000 invested because of the early start and extra years of compound growth.

Lesson: Start early or invest for longer.

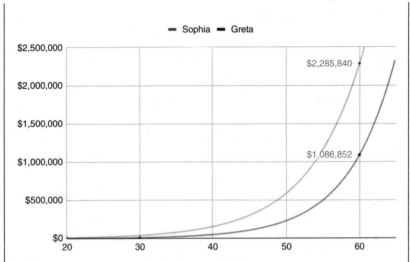

For illustrative purposes only. Assuming a moderate 7% return rate on your stock market investments. The historic annualized average return of the S&P 500 is around 10.5% since its inception in 1957.[2]

 Take Action

1. Participate in your employer-sponsored plans like a 401(k) or similar retirement plan. Choose your target-date fund.
2. Contribute at least the amount to get the full employer match, but aim to reach the IRS maximum limit.
3. Contribute to Roth IRAs. Invest the max allowed by the IRS.
4. Invest using a taxable brokerage account. Buy stocks, index funds, and ETFs directly in the stock market.

CHAPTER 18

Path 3: Debt Is Holding You Back

ebt takes up space in our minds that can be used in better ways.

If you're debt-free, you're sleeping better, you're more relaxed, and overall you are happier. Being debt-free means your future time belongs to you. It isn't allocated to working more hours just to pay the monthly minimums.

So, yes, I want you to be debt-free. You want to be debt-free. Consider prioritizing debt repayments as follows.

1. Unsecured credit cards

2. Personal loans

3. Auto loans

4. Student loans

5. Mortgages

Debt is a result of your credit usage.

Credit allows people to climb the socioeconomic ladder, but debt can affect your happiness and well-being. Studies show just the thought of debt can cause anxiety and psychological issues.[1] Your debt is holding you back and impacting your financial health.

Here are five tactics to pay off debt sooner.

1. Pay more towards credit card balances.

Credit card debt is costly, with revolving lines and high-interest rates. A small debt can grow uncontrollably if you only make the minimum monthly payments. Because installment loans have fixed payments, you'll want to target credit card balances with extra payments.

Each credit card statement includes a Payment Information box. Look at how adding a few extra dollars to the minimum payment can pay off credit card debt in three years. Estimated savings if the balance is paid off in about three years: $5,053.

Payment Information		
Payment Due Date January 11, 2023	For online and phone payments, the deadline is 8 p.m. ET.	
New Balance $3,410.61	Minimum Payment Due $114.00	
LATE PAYMENT WARNING: If we do not receive your minimum payment by your due date, you may have to pay a late fee of up to $40.		
MINIMUM PAYMENT WARNING If you make only the minimum payment each period, you will pay more in interest and it will take longer to pay off your balance. For example:		
If you make no additional charges using this card and each month you pay. . .	You will pay off the balance shown on this statement in about. . .	And you will end up paying an estimated total of. . .
Minimum Payment	18 Years	$10,014
$138	3 Years	$4,961
Estimated savings if balance is paid off in about 3 years: $5,053		

2. Negotiate to lower your interest rates.

Sometimes, there's a Catch-22. You want to apply for a consolidation loan but can't get approved because your debt-to-income (DTI) ratio is too high. So, you'll need to negotiate with your existing credit card companies and lenders. A lower APR can mean lower monthly payments and less interest paid in total.

3. Consolidate your credit cards.

If you're in good financial health, consider consolidating multiple credit cards to simplify repayment and lower the total cost of borrowing.

4. Transfer credit card balances.

A 0% balance transfer promotion can be a good tool to pay off debt sooner. A 0% interest rate on the transferred balance ensures your payments go directly towards the principal balance.

5. Refinance existing loans.

By refinancing, you can get a lower interest rate reducing the monthly payment amount. List all your large debts and contact the lenders. Ask them what options are available. Determine how much you can save by refinancing your mortgage, car loan, and student loans.

 Take Action

1. There is a lot to cover when it comes to achieving debt freedom. For more resources, visit phroogal.com/smilemoney.

CHAPTER **19**

Path 4: You Need to Make More Money

M any people believe they will never earn a million dollars in their life. You can earn a million dollars. Continue to challenge your perceptions about money, how income flows, and how much you can make.

The chart illustrates how a 6% annual salary increase can lead to million-dollar earnings. The increase can be a merit base increase from the same company or a salary increase from a new job.

	$30,000	$60,000	$90,000
10 Years	$395,000	$790,800	$1,186,300
20 Years	$1,103,600	$2,207,100	$3,310,700
30 Years	$2,371,700	$4,743,500	$7,115,200

It's not surprising that the more you're paid, the faster it is to earn $1 million. Getting paid more in your primary job is crucial.

Make more money in your career.

This can mean getting a pay raise, moving to a different position or department with a higher salary, or finding a higher-paying job in a new company. And as you learned from the Happy Mind chapter, continuous learning is good for happiness and your wallet. Your increased expertise can make you more valuable.

Get another income stream.

You need multiple sources of income. Having less reliance on a single source of income fosters peace of mind and well-being. The following are income categories offering many ways to earn and make money.

1. Active income

It's referred to as Earned Income by the IRS. You receive a paycheck or 1099 form for wages, salaries, commissions, and tips. It's active and material participation in business activity in which you exchange your time, skills, or energy for money. For example, you have active and earned income if you work as a salaried accountant or an hourly barista. Other examples include management, customer service, freelancers, teachers, construction workers, and so on.

2. Passive income

Your daily activity isn't required to make money. Passive income is from rental properties, royalties, and businesses where you don't actively participate. Passive income often requires an upfront investment of time, energy, and money but requires little effort in the future. Examples include rental properties, investing in a business, or receiving royalties for the use of your art, music, or book sales.

3. Portfolio income

By investing in the stock market, you're likely earning interest, receiving dividends, and making capital gains from selling shares. Some examples of portfolio income include investing in company stocks, depositing money into a savings account, and holding U.S. Savings Bonds.

You earn portfolio income by owning company stock that pays a quarterly dividend, saving money in an interest-bearing account, or selling a stock that has appreciated from $10 to $15 for a capital gain of $5.

Active income	Passive income	Portfolio income
• Your full-time job • Or part-time work • Driving others • Delivering packages • Cleaning homes • Babysitting • Completing surveys	• Rental property • Royalties from book • Online shop • Blogging • Content creator • Business profits	• Interest from savings accounts, certificates, etc. • Interest paid from loans • Dividends • Capital gains

I want you to consider this: there is no limit on how much you can make.

▼ Take Action

1. List your skills in your journal.
2. Determine what skill you can offer to others as a paid side gig.
3. Get an updated list of income stream ideas, visit phroogal.com/smilemoney.

Happy tip: Make as much as possible through your active income source and funnel the money into passive income opportunities.

CHAPTER **20**

Path 5: Start Investing Right Now

S tart sooner than later. Your future self will thank you.

"Compound interest is the eighth wonder of the world. He who understands it, earns it; he who doesn't, pays it," Albert Einstein is credited with saying.

Time is your most valuable resource allowing money to grow through compounding. Whether we're talking about compound growth or compound interest, the emphasis remains: your money will grow more because of the power of time.

Compounding is the interest you earn on the initial deposit and the interest you continue accumulating. In other words, it's earning interest-on-interest, which makes money grow. It works similarly with investments that grow based on interests, dividends, or capital gains.

Compounding Example: How Much Will You Have In Three Years?

Elena decided to open a savings account with an initial deposit of $100 on January 1 with an annual interest rate of 2%. How much will she have in three years?

If the bank offered 2% interest, then at the end of Year 1, Elena would have $102 on December 31. If she left the $102 for Year 2, Elena's account would grow to $104.04.

In this example, Elena earned interest on her initial $100 in Year 1. She then earned interest on the interest and initial deposit in Year 2. In Year 3, she would have $106.12.

Initial deposit	Year 1	Year 2	Year 3
$100.00	$102.00	$104.04	$106.12

Now imagine how much compounding would grow if the initial balance was larger, a higher interest rate, and a longer time horizon.

The Compounding Effect

Let's say Elena decided to invest $100 into an index fund that earns a 7% interest rate. She decided to automate $100 investments each month. Elena's money will continue to grow; by Year 20, her investments through compounding will surpass her principal contributions.

The longer your money is invested, the more it can grow. Time works in your favor. You can either start earlier or invest longer.

- Initial deposit: $100
- Monthly contributions: $100
- Average rate of return: 7%

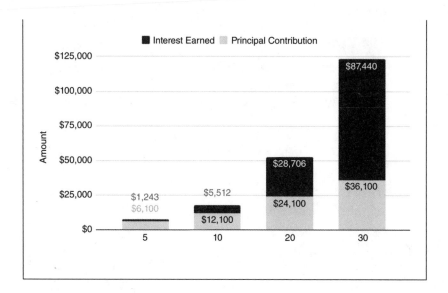

INVEST USING A TAXABLE BROKERAGE ACCOUNT

You're probably an investor already and don't know it. When you store money in a savings account that earns interest, then you're investing, albeit minimally. Investing in the stock market with a long-term strategy can lead to bigger gains and higher returns.

An investment account will not only provide you with a place to "store" your money but a way for it to "grow." You can invest in stocks and funds using an investment account. Doing so allows your money to grow through interest, dividends, or share price growth.

You don't need to be an expert to start investing.

There are simple rules: get started, remain consistent, diversify, increase contributions as income grows, and think long term. Build your wealth by investing in the stock market to achieve financial independence, pay for college, buy a home, and retire.

The Road to $1,000,000

The chart illustrates the benefit of starting to invest sooner. The earlier you start, the less you'll need to contribute monthly to reach $1,000,000.
For example, starting at age 20, you'll need to invest $283 monthly. If you wait until you're 30, you'll need to contribute about $300 more ($585) per month to reach the million-dollar goal by the time you're 65 years old.
Invest the monthly amounts to hit $1,000,000 by age 65.

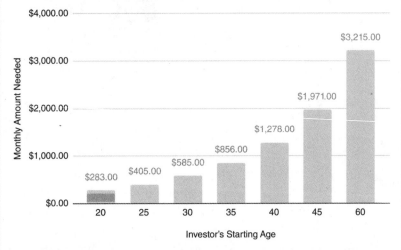

For illustrative purposes only. Assuming a moderate 7% return rate on your stock market investments. The historic annualized average return of the S&P 500 has been around 10.5% since its inception in 1957.[1]

Step 1: Open a Brokerage Account

Many online brokerages offer $0 minimums, no-commission trades, and other perks.

Option 1: a self-directed (DIY) brokerage account

With an online brokerage account, you can quickly start investing in stocks and funds. Evaluate brokerages based on minimums, costs, fees, and perks like investor research tools. A few brokerage account options are Fidelity, Charles Schwab, and Vanguard. They've been around for quite some time.

Option 2: a robo-advisor brokerage account

With a robo-advisor, you still have the option to invest in stocks and funds, but you'll get the most benefit from the investment services. These companies will ask about your goals and have you complete an onboarding process to build a portfolio. The cost of using robo-advisors is drastically lower than traditional investment management.

Whichever option you choose, you'll want to set up recurring investments.

Step 2: Choose an Investment Activity

For long-term growth, you can actively or passively buy stocks, index funds, exchange-traded funds (ETFs), and other securities.

Which investing approach is right for you?

It all depends on your risk tolerance, commitment to stock research, and execution of the trades. Perhaps, you want a simpler strategy: index funds are a good option for many because of their inherent diversification and lower risks.

GROWTH THROUGH SMALL INVESTMENTS

There is a misconception that you need a lot of money to start investing. Nothing can be further from the truth. Waiting to have lots of money before investing means you lose out on years of gains. While it can be daunting to begin investing, you can start small and grow into a significant portfolio. As a newbie investor, there are options to invest your first $100.

For example, Kayla wants to invest but doesn't have much left after bills. Calculating her expenses, she realized she could invest $50 or $100 each month. Let's look at what happens to smaller investments with the power of time.

The following chart shows how a small investment of $50 or $100 per month will grow in 40 years. It would benefit Kayla to choose to invest $100. She'll grow her portfolio by $130,000 more with an additional $24,000 investment.

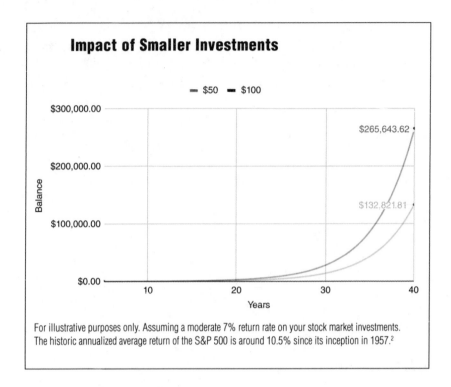

Impact of Smaller Investments

— $50 — $100

For illustrative purposes only. Assuming a moderate 7% return rate on your stock market investments. The historic annualized average return of the S&P 500 is around 10.5% since its inception in 1957.[2]

INVEST USING A ROTH IRA

You can open a Roth IRA—a tax-advantaged retirement account—through an online brokerage or robo-advisor.

Depending on when you start and how much you contribute can mean a larger retirement portfolio in your later years. Let's take three friends: Amelia, Matilda, and Clementine. They are all the same age, graduated college the same year, and got jobs that paid $60,000 per year. And that's where the similarities end.

- Amelia decided to contribute $6,000 (10% of her gross salary) into a Roth IRA annually until she is 60. Her total contributions are $240,000.

- Matilda decides to wait until she's 30 years old. She'll contribute $6,000 per year into a Roth IRA until she reaches the age of 60. Her total contributions are $180,000.

■ Clementine waits even further until she's 40 years old. She starts contributing $6,000 per year into a Roth IRA until the age of 60. Her total contributions are $120,000.

Look at the sizeable difference in portfolio growth.

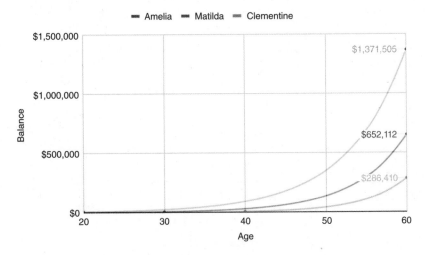

After 40 years, Amelia's $6,000 per year contribution has grown to $1,371,505. Matilda, who waited 10 years to start, has grown her portfolio to $652,112. And Clementine, who chose to wait, saw her 20 years of contributions grow to $286,410.

 Take Action

1. Open a brokerage account (visit phroogal.com/smilemoney for an updated list of low-cost online brokerage services).
2. Choose an investment activity.

Happy tip: Don't wait to start investing. Invest what you can. Utilize tax-advantaged accounts like a Roth IRA as part of your grow money strategy.

CHAPTER 21

Path 6:
Be Creditworthy,
Not Credit Hungry

C redit is a tool to help you make purchases before having money available. Not many people can afford to pay for big life-changing expenses without financing.

Being credit literate means understanding your financing options and how they affect your financial health. Credit literacy is knowing how to establish, build, and maintain good credit and understanding the factors impacting credit scores. Credit can be a book on its own, but I want to focus on credit for your peace of mind.

What does credit mean to you?

Credit can be used as leverage to achieve life goals. It enables you to buy a house that becomes a home for your family. And allows you to afford college, which leads to a higher-paying career. Credit can help you move up the socioeconomic ladder and lower the cost of living. Consider this:

- Getting lower interest rates to buy appreciating assets such as rental properties.

- Financing a new car with no down payment and 0% interest rate.
- Earning credit card reward points as you pay for basic living expenses.
- Accessing a credit line for expenses that emergency funds can't cover.

But many use credit to finance lifestyles and purchase depreciating assets like cars and televisions. Credit often leads to long-term debt. Debt becomes a heavy weight you carry, keeping you from leaping towards your life goals. You don't want debt!

Many have found success avoiding credit: I didn't. It created more complexity when traveling and dealing with business expenses. And here's a kicker: you need a credit history to sign an apartment lease, get a smartphone plan, and hook up utilities. And in some instances, credit history is used by companies for employment purposes.

You can't avoid credit, but you can learn to become creditworthy. There are two parts to credit: the report and score.

YOUR CREDIT REPORT

This is a data file of your financing relationships. It includes payment history, number of credit accounts, credit limits, and credit used, and any collection accounts, judgments, and liens. Three major credit bureaus collect this information: Experian, Equifax, and TransUnion.

Access your free credit report.

Go to AnnualCreditReport.com—the only federally mandated website jointly operated by the three bureaus. Request one credit report at a time. Then, review for accuracy and dispute incorrect information directly with the credit bureau through their website. After verifying the information and disputing inaccuracies in the first credit report, request a report from another bureau. And repeat the process.

Credit Report	Description
Personal information	Verify your name, social security number, date of birth, and current and previous addresses and phone numbers.
Employer information	Verify current and previous employers.
Credit accounts	Verify account status (closed, opened), creditor names, date opened, credit limits, balances, and payment history.
Inquiries	View soft and hard inquiries. Verify that hard inquiries are from your attempts to acquire credit.
Collection items	Verify for any outstanding collection reported.
Public records	Verify public records such as bankruptcy, civil suits, foreclosures, judgments, or liens.

YOUR CREDIT SCORE

The higher your credit score, the better you manage credit and debt. Credit scores make it easier for lenders to make loan decisions systematically. It can also mean that you experience less financial stress.

A credit score is a number between 300 and 850 that measures your creditworthiness. This score represents the answer from a mathematical formula that assigns numerical values to various pieces of information found in your credit report.

Credit scoring models are complex.

The exact information used by credit scoring providers to calculate your credit score is top secret, but there is some publicly available information. FICO, for instance, has shared the following: payment history (35%), amounts owed (30%), length of credit history (15%), types of credit (10%), and account inquiries (10%).

Improving Your Credit

Have You Paid Your Bills on Time?

Your payment history is a significant factor. A credit report that reflects one 30-day delinquency can drop your credit scores significantly. By how many points? We can't truly know. We know that payment history is 35% of your score: many late payments can lower your scores.

Are Your Credit Cards Maxed Out?

The amount of revolving credit is 30% of your credit score. It's what's referred to as credit utilization. Credit card balances that are near or at the credit limit are hurting your scores. There's a generally accepted recommendation: keep your balances below 30% of your limit. If you have to keep a balance, then follow the recommendation. However, my suggestion is to pay off credit card balances in full. You don't need to carry a balance.

How Long Have You Had Credit?

The longer you've had credit, the stronger your score can be. Basically, a lengthy credit history gives the scoring algorithms more data to use that predicts the likelihood of default or bankruptcy. Fifteen percent of your FICO score uses length to calculate scores. It's beneficial to start your credit history sooner, but that doesn't mean accumulating debt or holding onto it for extended periods of time.

Have You Applied for New Credit Lately?

Credit applications are also used to calculate your scores. Applying for credit is considered a credit inquiry and is factored into your score. Too many inquiries can negatively impact your credit. There's a difference between soft and hard inquiries, where hard hits mean you applied for credit (and may or may not have been approved). There are exceptions to this rule concerning shopping for auto loans and mortgages.

How Many and What Types of Accounts Are Reported?

If it wasn't any more confusing, scores factor in the mixture of accounts. Basically, they want to see different types of credit, such as credit cards, loans, mortgages, and so forth.

Do You Have Any Outstanding Uncollected Debt?

Credit reports showing public liens and collections can impact your score and ability to get future credit. Verify these records, and settle or dispute inaccuracies.

Do You Have a Bankruptcy?

Bankruptcy is a legal protection that some have used to relieve the pressure of insurmountable debt. It's important to understand that bankruptcy isn't an end but a beginning: an opportunity to renew. Bankruptcy is reported for 7 to 10 years, depending on the Chapter of the Bankruptcy Code that was filed, and significantly impacts credit scores. Fortunately, you can reestablish your credit with a secured credit card or secured loan.

 Take Action

1. Request your credit report from annualcreditreport.com.
2. Review your report for accuracy.
3. Download a free credit report monitoring app with a credit score.

For an updated list of the best credit apps and tools, visit phroogal.com/smilemoney.

CHAPTER 22

Path 7: For Your Protection, Please

We often think about earning or investing money, but rarely does the conversation enter the realm of protecting money. As you create wealth, you must consider how to protect your prized possessions—your life, family, and assets.

We often don't think about preventive measures that lower future financial stress. I want you to consider these four areas.

PROTECT YOUR IDENTITY

With the growing number of data breaches, keeping your personal information safe continues to be challenging.

- *Monitor your credit report regularly.* Use a free credit report monitoring service to help you.
- *Enroll in an identity theft protection service.* Your personal information is more than your credit report. If you're a victim of ID theft, you'll have a service to help you regain control.

- *Safeguard your social security number.* Don't share your number with anyone who isn't authorized. Always ask why your social security number is required.
- *Use credit cards for purchases.* With credit cards, you get more legal protection compared to debit cards.

PROTECT YOURSELF FROM SCAMS

Many scammers are looking to take your money or use your identity for nefarious reasons.

- *Be socially aware.* Don't share too much personal information on social media like the financial services you use or post answers to questions that can be used to guess your password.
- *Don't fall prey to email and phishing scams.* They ask you to click on a link and provide your login information. Verify website URLs and don't click on links from unsolicited emails, text or direct messages.
- *Watch out for phone scams.* The U.S. federal agencies like the IRS or Social Security Administration will not call you or threaten you with arrest if you don't pay them.
- *Save yourself from social scams.* Scammers use social media to get you to click on links that either download viruses or ask for your login and passwords. Be wary of direct message scams too.

PROTECT YOUR ASSETS

You don't need a lot of insurance, you just need the correct insurance and the right amount to protect yourself from unforeseen hardships and losses. Insurance is really about mitigating risks.

- *Protect your stuff.* Review your homeowner's or renters' insurance to verify how much of your personal stuff is covered.
- *Protect your loved ones.* Consider how much life insurance they'll need to cover your financial obligations if you pass.

■ *Protect your income.* With disability insurance, you can supplement the loss of your income when you're injured or sick and unable to work. Disability insurance is often offered through employers and can be purchased personally as well.

■ *Protect your senior years.* You may want to consider long-term care insurance to help you in your later years to prevent nursing home stays or home health care support from draining your savings accounts.

Types of Insurance

■ Auto insurance
■ Disability insurance
■ Health insurance
■ Homeowner's insurance
■ Life insurance
■ Renter's insurance
■ Business insurance

PROTECT YOUR EARNINGS

You need to have a tax strategy to lower tax liabilities. For most people, taxes are an afterthought and are only a topic of conversation in the first three months of the year. Understanding how taxes affect your finances is vital to your financial health.

■ *Evaluate your withholding.* You tell your employer how much tax to withhold from your paycheck using the W-4 form. But we often don't look at it again after the first payday.

■ *Review past tax returns.* Do an inventory of past deductions, credits, and adjustments and determine how they affect your taxes.

■ *Retirement planning is tax planning.* Take advantage of tax-advantaged retirement accounts: employer plans like 401(k)s and 403(b)s, and IRAs like Roths.

PROTECT YOUR LEGACY

With some preparation, you can lessen stress by outlining your goals for your money.

Think about your future and what can happen if you get sick or after your death. Ask yourself who will decide for you or carry out your wishes and determine how you'll divide your estate. Although it may be difficult to have this conversation, it's important to communicate with your loved ones way in advance.

- *Last will and testament.* It's important you have your wishes written down and witnessed by a professional. Unless you draft your own will, the government has a default plan for your assets.
- *Trusts.* A trust can be used to distribute your assets after your death. It's more often used to minimize taxes and avoid probate.
- *Powers of attorney.* Have a plan to protect yourself if you're ill, hospitalized, or unable to make decisions. Consider these types of power of attorney: financial power of attorney, health care power of attorney, and living will.
- *Joint tenancy with rights of survivorship.* When you hold a title for an asset with someone else, like a house or car, then your stake of the asset transfers directly to the surviving owner.

YOU'RE NOT ALONE

Money can buy happiness by affording you access to highly qualified and knowledgeable professionals. Protect your inner peace by hiring experts to help you with specific financial needs. You can work with financial advisors, certified financial planners (CFP®), certified public accountants (CPA), accredited financial counselors (AFC®), insurance brokers, and more. Ask your family and friends for referrals. Do your research to verify their experience and credentials.

Take Action

1. Add beneficiaries to accounts. Make sure you name a beneficiary and contingent beneficiary to every financial account, retirement plan, and insurance policy. When you name a beneficiary for these accounts, plans, and policies, they skip probate. These accounts automatically become "payable on death" to the named beneficiary.

Happy tip: There's a lot to cover to help protect your financial health and peace of mind. Visit phroogal.com/smilemoney for more resources on identity protection, insurance, taxes, and estate planning.

CHAPTER **23**

Path 8: Your Ultimate Safety Net

Having a cash reserve is essential to financial freedom. Since your primary income may come from investments in the stock market, you'll need a substantial amount of cash that isn't tied to market fluctuations. Having a cash reserve can cover your monthly living expenses as you ride out the market downturns.

My cash reserve helped me through the pandemic quarantine. I saved 12 months of expenses, which lessened the stress when my income was disrupted due to event cancellations.

Maintain your peace of mind with a 12-month cash reserve.

Your cash reserve should carry less risk and remain accessible. Therefore, store your funds in a high-yield savings account, certificates (CDs), and a money market account or a combination of the three. Sure, you won't maximize your returns if you have that much money in a savings account, but the cash reserve is about securing your independence.

Don't be concerned about fully maximizing returns on a cash reserve as you would for investments. The goal is to experience less financial stress related to investment performance during stock market crashes or economic recessions.

Securing Your Financial Independence

Use your monthly living expenses to determine how much to save. Your cash reserve will include 12–24 months of living expenses.

Monthly expenses × Months = Cash reserve goal

For example, your monthly income is $4,000 with monthly expenses of $3,500.

Monthly expenses	Multiply	Months	Equals	Cash reserve goal
$3,500	×	12	=	$42,000

 Take Action

1. Calculate your cash reserve total. After doing so, you might feel overwhelmed. Understand the total is your target amount. Start by transferring a small amount each pay period to help you reach your goal.

Happy tip: Focus on your opportunity fund goal (shared in Step 1) before working on the Cash Reserve.

CHAPTER **24**

Path 9:
Independence Is
Your Birthright

Even if you love your job, have a plan to make work optional. Independence gives you the freedom to work on other parts of your life. You owe it to yourself to own your time.

Achieve financial freedom by becoming financially independent.

Financial independence is for everyone, and you can achieve this lofty goal. It will not be easy, but the challenge itself may expand your understanding of your true capabilities. Although mass media coverage focuses on people who retire from work after amassing a sizable nest egg, the truth is: that financial independence is a matter of lifestyle, income, and math.

"I reached financial independence in my 30s," says James Cuevas, "I was contributing to my retirement and investment accounts and one day realized I had enough to retire."

James, 38, is a former financial advisor who managed high-net-worth clients with assets of $3 million or more. He was laid off from his job due to a merger that saw his position eliminated with a brokerage firm. I interviewed James—who is my cousin—about his journey.

"It took me for a shock," added James. Although he was financially ready to retire, he wasn't ready to stop working. But his financial independence allowed him to take much-needed time off. Instead of rushing to find a new job, he spent months in Europe and an entire year in Mexico City.

"What did financial independence offer you?" I asked.

Without hesitation, James replied, "It gave me time to pause. I was caught in the chase. But I had this nagging feeling of wanting to do something else for some time."

"What did the pause do for you?" I said curiously.

"The pause gave me time to reflect and figure out what's next. What do I want to do with my life? Being able to support myself financially, I now had the time I didn't have before to figure it out," James responded.

Achieving financial independence is almost entirely about regaining your time.

Financial independence is when you have enough money to cover your basic needs and luxuries. Your monthly living expenses are covered through savings accounts and income generated from assets or investments without the need to work or earn income from a job. The sign of financial independence is having sufficient wealth when working is a choice, not a requirement: it's a work-optional lifestyle.

Many achieve financial independence later in life through traditional retirement using 401(k)s, IRAs, pensions, and Social Security benefits. And some achieve this through an intentional and detailed financial plan of saving and investing.

Financial independence is about having the "right" amount of wealth, to no longer be dependent on a job to pay for living expenses. It sounds like retirement, but the main difference is timing and when you get to live off your wealth.

James relies only on investment returns to afford his living expenses. He shared that financial independence is about regaining time and having more options.

Your path to financial independence leads to *time wealth*. When you can confidently cover all your expenses without working, you regain control over your time and what you do within that time. You can spend that time with loved ones, work on passion projects, volunteer, pursue a new profession, or even start a new business.

Financial independence allows you to walk a nontraditional path. You can find yourself traveling the world and gaining new experiences that expand your understanding of what's possible.

In his travels, James met dozens of people who asked him how he could support his life. He realized so many didn't have a basic understanding of personal finance. But his experience working with high-net-worth professionals also informed him about the lack of financial planning is commonplace.

James shared that the high-net-worth clients he's worked with were highly paid professionals. Most saw themselves working until they couldn't, but they all wanted to be financially secure. His approach to them was to find a balance between their financial and life goals. After returning to the United States, James started Flip on Finance to help first-generation Americans reach financial independence to own their time and live their best lives.

"So, how can more people regain their time?" I asked.

"It's a matter of lifestyle and math," he replied, "there's a calculation we can all do to determine how much is needed. Wealth is really a number. But what holds back people I've worked with is their lifestyle."

What can you do to get started?

CHALLENGE YOUR LIFESTYLE CHOICES

You've made financial decisions to cultivate a lifestyle. Now, you'll need to determine if it's the lifestyle you still desire.

During an interview, Saundra Davis, the founder of the Financial Fitness Coach (FFC®) certification program, shared, "There's a big difference between lifestyle and living expenses." For example, a living expense is housing. The cost of housing varies widely in different parts of the country. On the other hand, lifestyle expenses are personal choices.

"Lifestyle expenses are the way you choose to live, and living expenses are the cost of living in an area. You can cut back on lifestyle choices, but there might not be much you can do with living expenses," she added.

Lifestyle expense	Living expense
▪ The way in which you live ▪ Includes interests, likes, needs and wants, your feelings and motives	▪ The cost of living in a particular area ▪ Includes income and economic opportunities in a community or area

Perhaps, you've chosen a more expensive apartment with city views. You may be able to reduce lifestyle expenses by choosing an apartment without views, but you can't control the standard housing cost of a given community.

"And you might not want to leave the community because of what it offers socially and environmentally that supports your well-being," says Saundra.

Be mindful of lifestyle inflation.

It happens when your spending increases as your income rises. Lifestyle inflation often becomes greater every time you get a raise. There is nothing wrong with upgrading your life as your income increases. But an unintended effect may lead to living paycheck to paycheck to keep up appearances. This can make it challenging to save for retirement, get out of debt, or reach financial independence. Lifestyle inflation can be why people (you, maybe) cannot reach their goals.

What can you do to lower lifestyle expenses without depriving yourself of comfort?

Saundra recommends doing an audit of your current lifestyle. "Ask yourself, 'what are the essentials needed for a happy life?' The nonnegotiables."

Basically, you can only cut expenses so much before it starts impacting your well-being. There has to be a level of lifestyle that fosters joy and happiness.

HOW TO REACH FINANCIAL INDEPENDENCE

"You'll need to calculate your financial independence number," says James when speaking with clients. "It's the amount of money you need to pay for your expenses without running out of money."

Once you have the amount of money saved and invested equal to your financial independence (FI) number, you can happily call yourself financially independent. Achieving financial independence may be challenging, but it's not impossible. You can estimate how much money you'll need with a straightforward calculation.

There are four steps in determining your FI number.

- Step 1: Calculate your spending.
- Step 2: Calculate your financial independence number.
- Step 3: Calculate your safe withdrawal rate.
- Step 4: Calculate the years to financial independence.

Step 1: Calculate Your Spending

The first step is to calculate your annual spending. You're ahead if you've created a budget and monitored your cash flow. You can use your cash flow expense column to calculate your financial independence (FI) number.

Your Annual Expenses Total

1. Start by calculating your monthly expenses.
2. And then multiply that amount by 12.
3. Add your monthly expenses, including periodic and quarterly payments and annual premiums, to get your annual expenses total.

For example, if your total monthly expenses are $4,167, your annual expenses are $50,000.

Monthly expenses	Multiply	12	Equals	Annual expenses total
$4,167	×	12	=	$50,000
$	×	12	=	$

Take action: Calculate your annual expenses.
Happy tip: With fewer monthly expenses, your financial independence number will be lower.

Step 2: Calculate Your Financial Independence Number

To calculate your FI number, you can choose your current annual expenses total or use a desired annual spending amount. Then, use the rule of 25, which states you're ready to retire when you've saved 25 times your planned annual spending.

Your Financial Independence Number

To get your FI number, look at your desired spending, and multiply that by 25.

For example, your annual expenses is $50,000, then you'll need $1,250,000 ($50,000 × 25) saved.

The calculation for the Rule of 25 is as follows:

Financial independence number = Yearly spending × 25

Yearly spending	Multiply	25	Equals	FI number
$50,000	×	25	=	$1,250,000
$	×	25	=	$

Take action: Calculate your FI number.

Happy tip: Housing is a big expense. You might consider paying off your mortgage, refinancing, downsizing, or moving to a lower-cost living area to lower your FI number.

Step 3: Choose Your Safe Withdrawal Rate

The safe withdrawal rate (also referred to as SWR) is a conservative method that retirees use to determine how much money can be withdrawn from accounts each year without running out of money for the rest of their lives.

James said, "The safe withdrawal rate method instructs people to take out a small percentage between 3% and 4% of their investment portfolios." The withdrawal percentage is from the Trinity Study[1] and is used to mitigate worst-case scenarios.

The 4% rule says you can safely withdraw 4% of the value of your investments during your first year of financial independence. You can withdraw the same dollar amount adjusted for inflation in the following years. The Trinity Study found the 4% rule applies through all market ups and downs. Withdrawing no more than 4% of your initial investments each year, your assets should last for the rest of your life.

How Much Can You Withdraw?

With the previous example, the $1,250,000 investment portfolio allows you to withdraw $50,000 per year indefinitely using the 4% rule or safe withdrawal rate.

Investment portfolio	Multiply	SWR	Equals	Safe withdrawal amount
$1,250,000	×	0.04 or 4%	=	$50,000
$	×	0.04 or 4%	=	$

Take action: Calculate your safe withdrawal amount

Interestingly, you can use the 4% rule to calculate your FI number as well. If you do the math, you'll notice that the Rule of 25 and the 4% are quite similar. Both require investing for long-term growth.

Calculating FI Number Using the 4% Rule

To calculate your FI number, take your annual expenses total and divide it by your safe withdrawal rate.

For example, use the 4% safe withdrawal rate with your annual expenses total of $40,000.

The calculation is:

Financial independence number = Yearly spending/SWR

Using the example:

$$\$40,000/0.04 = \$1,000,000$$

Based on this example, you'll need to accumulate $1,000,000 in your portfolio to reach financial independence.

Annual expense total	Divided	Safe withdrawal rate	Equals	FI number
$40,000	÷	0.04	=	$1,000,000
$	÷	0.04	=	$

Take action: Calculate your FI number using the SWR.
Happy tip: Your portfolio can include retirement accounts, investable assets (brokerages, stocks, etc.), pensions, rental properties, business ownership stakes, etc.

Step 4: Calculate the Years to Financial Independence

Once you have your FI number, you can calculate how many years it will take to achieve financial independence. If you're looking to cut back the number of years and accelerate your path to FI, you'll want to invest more money to reach your goal.

Years to Financial Independence

Years to FI = (FI Number − Existing portfolio amount)/Yearly savings

Existing Portfolio Amounts: the total amount of money already saved that includes retirement accounts, investable accounts (brokerage, stocks, etc.), pensions, and other savings accounts.
Yearly Savings: the amount of money you invest per month multiplied by 12 months.
For example, using the $1,000,000 FI number and having an existing investment portfolio of $250,000 with $25,000 in yearly investments.

($1,000,000 − $250,000)/$25,000 = 30 Years to FI

If your FI number is $1,000,000 and you've already saved $250,000, then all you'll need is $750,000. And by investing $25,000 per year, it will take you 30 years to reach your FI number.

FI number	Minus	Existing portfolio amount	Divided	Yearly investing amount	Equals	Years to FI
$1,000,000	–	$250,000	÷	$25,000	=	30
$	–	$	÷	$	=	

Take action: Calculate your years to FI.
Happy tip: You can accelerate reaching financial independence by making more money and increasing your investing contributions.

 Take Action

1. Calculate your financial independence number.
2. Calculate how long it will take you to reach FI.
3. Find more tips and resources by visiting www.phroogal.com/smilemoney.

SMILE MONEY STEPS CONCLUSION

Congrats, you've completed the multilayered Smile Money Paths to reach financial independence. Revisit the paths you need more help with and visit phroogal.com for additional resources.

- Path 1: Save for the unexpected.
- Path 2: You're going to retire one day.
- Path 3: Debt is holding you back.
- Path 4: You need to make more money.
- Path 5: Start investing right now.
- Path 6: Be creditworthy, not credit hungry.
- Path 7: For your protection, please.
- Path 8: Your ultimate safety net.
- Path 9: Independence is your birthright.

ACHIEVING FINANCIAL FREEDOM

Becoming financially free shifts your attention to the more important things in life. You now have time and the mental bandwidth to create the life you've dreamed of. You have more options to choose happiness. You'll own your time to do as you wish, including working on meaningful projects.

The following happy tips can help accelerate your path to living financially free.

- Tip 1: Spend way less than you earn.
- Tip 2: Eliminate debt.
- Tip 3: Diversify and multiply income streams.
- Tip 4: Buy appreciating and income-generating assets.
- Tip 5: Stay consistent and keep investing.

Tip 1: Spend Way Less than You Earn

In other words, lower your monthly expenses and cut your discretionary spending way down. Not everyone seeking financial independence is cheap, but they take extreme measures to control spending. With every penny saved, they then have the potential to grow.

You accelerate your FI timeline when you save more than you spend. There is a dual benefit to lowering your expenses and spending less: (1) the lower your expenses, the more money you save, and (2) having smaller lifestyle expenses means the money you need to save is lower.

But a happy life isn't about deprivation but the reallocation of your money to the most important things.

What non value-added expenses can you eliminate?

Tip 2: Eliminate Debt

The goal is to eliminate monthly debt payments to decrease the total monthly expense of your lifestyle. Regardless of how you've borrowed, debt is an obligation. Having debt allocates more of your time to work rather than fun. For instance, making $25 per hour and having a $30,000 car loan means 1,200 hours of your life or 30 work weeks is tied to that vehicle. That's how much time is no longer yours.

How will you change your relationship with credit?

Tip 3: Diversify and Multiply Income Streams

Having multiple income streams can support financial well-being. You don't want to be dependent on one source. You can achieve financial independence with your investments, but ideally, various sources will give you more freedom. You don't want to be financially independent but dependent solely on stock investment income. Diversification and multiplication of income streams will make you more secure and offer more choices.

How many income streams do you have?

Tip 4: Buy Appreciating and Income-Generating Assets

Once expenses are reduced and you have additional income streams, start using that money to invest in assets that appreciate or generate income. Essentially, you continue to buy assets that make money and use the earnings from those assets to buy more income-generating assets. Rinse and repeat.

Invest in the stock market.

The stock market has a historically long-term track record of growth and is used by many financially independent people to build wealth. Building a portfolio invested heavily in stocks may be necessary to earn the kind of returns you need. But, choosing index funds may be the better option. Index funds and exchange-traded funds (ETFs) allow you to purchase many companies trading in the stock market in a single transaction.

Investing in index funds and ETFs is a simpler path to wealth: it saves time. And it is recommended by many people who've reached financial independence. You don't have to research companies extensively, chase flashy finance news, or use gut instincts to figure out which stock to buy.

Invest in rental properties.

Many financially independent people are real estate investors. They've shared that these investments provide a steady monthly income. You do need to be conscious of the costs of property maintenance and repairs when you sign up for this. If you prefer less work, investing in REITs (real estate investment trusts) might be a better option.

What assets will you buy?

Tip 5: Stay Consistent and Keep Investing

With investing, you need to be consistent through the good and bad years. It can be challenging to invest when the market is down. Downturns in the market can be a buying opportunity.

Warren Buffett, one of the most successful investors of all time, once said investors would be wise to be "fearful when others are greedy, and greedy when others are fearful." When the market is rallying and stocks are rising, you'll most likely overpay on an investment.

To keep your peace, follow a simpler investing strategy, automate your investments, remain consistent, and persist through all the market ups and downs. You can benefit from dollar-cost averaging by automating investing.

Why is achieving financial freedom important to you?

Conclusion: Choose Happiness

Congratulations! You've done it and read through three books. I want you to take a minute and savor this moment. Not many people finish entire books, but here you are at the end, which is just the beginning of your journey into better health, wealth, and financial freedom.

I want you to take everything you've learned—the Happy Dimensions and Smile Money Paths—and think about your life: where is it today, and where do you want to be tomorrow?

I want you to use the dimensions and think, feel, imagine, hope, and dream of your happy life. Let the dimensions guide you into envisioning your happiness and well-being.

What is the vision for your happy life?

A vision considers your thoughts and feelings and your hopes and dreams. A vision is the bigger picture of who you'll be, how you'll feel, and what you'll be doing. It's where you want your life to be. You can't get to where you want to be if you don't know where you're going. Your core values will inform your vision for life.

Understand that no amount of money will be enough to get you to *destination: unknown*. You need a direction, a vision, to compel you.

Sometimes people will ask me to jump into the tactics. Sure, tactics are great. You've read plenty of them, but often tactics are not enough to change the trajectory of your life. You need direction (vision) and an understanding of your motivations (core values) to set the right goals—goals that turn lofty visions into concrete objectives.

I purposefully placed vision-creation in the conclusion. I want you to envision your life with all the knowledge you've gained. What kind of person are you? How will you live?

How do you envision living?

YOUR HAPPY VISION STATEMENT

A personal vision statement helps you decide what goals are important. You're not easily distracted by shiny new things when you clearly envision where you'd like to go.

Start thinking about a vision for your life. Refer to the happy dimensions and your core values in the Happy Spirit exercise. Answer the following questions:

- What type of person are you in the future?
- What kind of life are you living 10 years from now? In retirement?
- What do you enjoy doing? How do you feel doing what you enjoy?
- What makes you happy? What are the essentials in your life?
- Who do you want to be surrounded by? What kind of people fulfill you?
- What would people remember about you or say when you're no longer around?
- What do you want to create in the world?

Write down your answers in your journal.

My vision statement: To be happy, healthy, and secure. Spending my time discovering the meaning of life, exploring the corners of the world and the inner depths of my mind, immersed in experiences, and sharing the wonders with others. To serve a purpose that fulfills my mind, heart, and spirit. Surrounded by deep, meaningful friendships and connections.

This may sound broad, but my vision statement includes my core values and hits all dimensions. My vision helps me prioritize exploration through travel and meaningful connections with family and friends. It helps me choose projects and opportunities that align better with my life goals. For example, my goal of sharing experiences motivates me to write articles and create videos. And my financial goals are focused on time freedom and less on material accumulation.

Once you have a vision statement. I want you to keep it top of mind. Read it every day. Memorize it. Take a photo and make it your phone's screen saver. Print, frame, and hang it up where you can see it daily. Feel free to share it out to the world using #thesmilelifestyle. Get clever.

Happiness is a choice: choose to take action to live the life you've envisioned—your happy life.

HAPPY MONEY HAPPY LIFE KEY LESSONS

Book I: In Pursuit of Happiness	
You can choose to be happy.	
Money can buy happiness, but money *isn't* happiness.	
Money buys happiness by impacting health and wellness.	
Improve your well-being and experience long-term happiness.	

Book II: Happy Life	
You only live once; make it a happy life.	
Happy Money	Living financially free.
Happy Work	Rewire; don't retire.
Happy Mind	Invest in yourself and learn continually.
Happy Heart	Memories appreciate; stuff depreciates.
Happy Body	Be kind to your body; it's priceless.
Happy Social	Connections are your lifeline.
Happy Space	Free your space and yourself.
Happy Spirit	Serve a purpose, not a purchase.

Book III: Happy Money	
Money is the tool to achieve goals.	
Part 1: Money Beliefs	
Tell me what you want	What you really want.
You really want to create	Money isn't the end goal.
You really want wealth	Building wealth isn't a selfish act.
You really want more time	Time is a finite resource.

Part 2: Money Vitals	
1. Net worth	Net worth is your security number.
2. Cash flow	Cash flow is your safety number.
3. Income number	Income number is your scalability number.
4. Credit score	Credit score is your credibility number.
5. Debt-to-income	Debt-to-income is your movability number.

Part 3: Money Journey	
Path 1: Save for the unexpected	Your emergency savings plan.
Path 2: You're going to retire one day	Contribute to retirement accounts.
Path 3: Debt is holding you back	Prioritize debt payoff.
Path 4: You need to make more money	Multiply and diversify your income.
Path 5: Start investing right now	Make money with money.
Path 6: Be creditworthy, not credit hungry	Use credit as leverage for wealth building.
Path 7: For your protection, please	Protect your most prized possessions.
Path 8: Your ultimate safety net	Build a cash reserve for peace of mind.
Path 9: Independence is your birthright	Reach financial independence.

A Poetic Affirmation

My happy money truths.
I will save.
I will invest.
I will pay off debt.
I will spend a little less.
And make a bit more.
But I will live.
Not just alive.
Willing
and Living.
A happy life.
Less money worries.
And more life stories.

Notes

CHAPTER 1

1. "World Happiness Report," https://worldhappiness.report/ed/2022/happiness-benevolence-and-trust-during-covid-19-and-beyond/#ranking-of-happiness-2019-2021.
2. "High Income Improves Evaluation of Life But Not Emotional Well-Being," *PNAS*, https://www.pnas.org/doi/10.1073/pnas.1011492107.
3. "Experienced Well-Being Rises with Income, Even above $75,000 Per Year," *PNAS*, https://www.pnas.org/doi/10.1073/pnas.2016976118.
4. "Time, Money and Happiness," *ScienceDirect*, https://faculty.wharton.upenn.edu/wp-content/uploads/2016/01/Mogilner-Norton-Time-Money-Happiness-Current-Opinion-in-Psychology-2016_2.pdf.
5. "Hedonic Treadmill," Wikipedia, https://en.wikipedia.org/wiki/Hedonic_treadmill.
6. https://link.springer.com/article/10.1007/s11482-019-09763-8.

CHAPTER 2

1. "Survey Reveals Tension in How People Think about Finances," Capital One CreditWise, https://www.capitalone.com/about/newsroom/survey-reveals-tension-between-financial-stress-and-optimistic-financial-outlook-among-us-consumers/.
2. "Conceptualizing Health and Financial Wellness," The Forum, https://dr.lib.iastate.edu/server/api/core/bitstreams/a4a0e5e9-9c88-4b0a-8124-a8743eca33b6/content.
3. "Measuring Financial Well-Being," Consumer Financial Protection Bureau, https://www.consumerfinance.gov/data-research/research-reports/financial-well-being-scale/.
4. "Stress Effects on the Body," American Psychological Association, https://www.apa.org/topics/stress/body.

CHAPTER 3

1. Oprah Winfrey, *What I Know for Sure* (New York: Flatiron Books, 2014), p. 167.
2. *New York Times*, http://www.nytimes.com/2010/04/18/magazine/18FOB-onlanguage-t.html.
3. Instagram, @iyanlavanzant, https://www.instagram.com/tv/CfHIu15rFM4/?igshid=YmMyMTA2M2Y%3D.

CHAPTER 4

1. CaseyNeistat channel, YouTube, https://youtu.be/ROfBLx6bLZI.
2. "If Money Doesn't Make You Happy Then You're Probably Not Spending It Right," Harvard University, https://scholar.harvard.edu/files/danielgilbert/files/if-money-doesnt-make-you-happy.nov-12-20101.pdf.
3. "The Sharp Spikes of Poverty," Harvard Business School, https://www.hbs.edu/ris/Publication%20Files/FinancialScarcity_SPPS_accepted_November1_2021_06f87dd3-4474-4c92-88d1-a5c6b63a2eaa.pdf.
4. "Revisiting the Sustainable Happiness Model and Pie Chart," *The Journal of Positive Psychology*, http://sonjalyubomirsky.com/files/2019/11/Sheldon-Lyubomirsky-2019.pdf.

CHAPTER 5

1. "Financial Security, More than Money Alone, May Be the Key To Happiness," Princeton University, https://www.princeton.edu/news/2009/03/17/financial-security-more-money-alone-may-be-key-happiness-princeton-study-says.
2. "Positive Thinking, Stop Negative Self-Talk to Reduce Stress," Mayo Clinic, https://www.mayoclinic.org/healthy-lifestyle/stress-management/in-depth/positive-thinking/art-20043950.
3. "Optimism and Its Impact on Mental and Physical Wellbeing," National Library of Medicine, https://www.ncbi.nlm.nih.gov/pmc/articles/PMC2894461/.
4. "Does Giving Make You Happier? Or Do Happier People Give?," Utah State University, https://www.usu.edu/science/discovery/fall-2017/does-giving-make-you-happy.

CHAPTER 6

1. National Library of Medicine, https://www.ncbi.nlm.nih.gov/pmc/articles/PMC6481914/.
2. *Harvard Business Review*, https://hbr.org/2018/11/9-out-of-10-people-are-willing-to-earn-less-money-to-do-more-meaningful-work.

CHAPTER 7

1. Money and Mental Health Policy Institute, https://www.moneyandmentalhealth.org/money-and-mental-health-facts/.
2. "Mental Wellbeing Inherently Connected to Financial Wellness," Purdue University, https://www.purdue.edu/newsroom/purduetoday/releases/2021/Q1/mental-well-being-inherently-connected-to-financial-wellness.html.
3. Anne Craig, "Discovery of 'Thought Worms' Opens Window into the Mind," *Queens Gazette*, https://www.queensu.ca/gazette/stories/discovery-thought-worms-opens-window-mind.

CHAPTER 8

1. Clever Real Estate, https://listwithclever.com/research/best-and-worst-cities-for-commmuters-2022/.
2. Rejournals.com, https://rejournals.com/self-storage-is-on-a-growth-kick-and-its-not-slowing-down.

CHAPTER 9

1. American Psychological Association, https://www.apa.org/topics/stress/chronic.
2. "The Benefits of Slumber," National Institute of Health, https://newsinhealth.nih.gov/2013/04/benefits-slumber.
3. TechNavio, https://www.technavio.com/report/athleisure-market-industry-analysis.

CHAPTER 10

1. "Loneliness and Isolation during the COVID-19 Pandemic," National Library of Medicine, https://www.ncbi.nlm.nih.gov/pmc/articles/PMC7306546/.

2. "Do Social Ties Affect Our Health?" National Institutes of Health, https://newsinhealth.nih.gov/2017/02/do-social-ties-affect-our-health.
3. "Spousal Similarities in Cardiometabolic Risk Factors," *Atherosclerosis*, https://www.atherosclerosis-journal.com/article/S0021-9150(21)01310-1/fulltext.
4. "Why Lottery Winners May Make Their Neighbors Go Broke," *Washington Post*, https://www.washingtonpost.com/news/wonk/wp/2016/03/02/why-lottery-winners-may-make-their-neighbors-go-broke/.
5. Thrive Global, https://thriveglobal.com/stories/relationships-happiness-well-being-life-lessons/.
6. "Spending Money on Others Promotes Happiness," Research Gate, https://www.researchgate.net/publication/5494996_Spending_Money_on_Others_Promotes_Happiness.

CHAPTER 11

1. *Harvard Business Review*, https://hbr.org/2019/03/the-case-for-finally-cleaning-your-desk.
2. "The Dark Side of Home: Assessing 'Possession' Clutter on Subjective Well-Being," Science Direct, https://www.sciencedirect.com/science/article/abs/pii/S0272494416300159.
3. "Life at Home in the Twenty-First Century," UCLA Cotsen Institute of Archaeology, https://ioa.ucla.edu/press/life-at-home.
4. "Interactions of Top-Down and Bottom-Up Mechanisms in Human Visual Cortex," National Library of Medicine, https://pubmed.ncbi.nlm.nih.gov/21228167/.
5. *Princeton Alumni Weekly*, https://paw.princeton.edu/article/psychology-your-attention-please.
6. "Forest Bathing Is Great for Your Health," *Time*, https://time.com/5259602/japanese-forest-bathing/.

CHAPTER 12

1. IRI, https://www.iriworldwide.com/en-us/insights/publications/self-care-trends.
2. *Science Magazine*, https://happylabubc.files.wordpress.com/2010/12/spending-money-on-others-promotes-happiness.pdf.
3. *Time*, https://time.com/collection/guide-to-happiness/4070299/secret-to-happiness/.

4. "Relationships between Mindfulness, Purpose in Life, Happiness, Anxiety, and Depression," National Library of Medicine, https://www.ncbi.nlm.nih.gov/pmc/articles/PMC7908241/.

5. "Self-Affirmation Activates Brain Systems," National Library of Medicine, https://www.ncbi.nlm.nih.gov/pmc/articles/PMC4814782/.

6. "Giving Thanks Can Make You Happier," Harvard Health Publishing, https://www.health.harvard.edu/healthbeat/giving-thanks-can-make-you-happier.

BOOK III

1. "Financial Capability, Income and Psychological Wellbeing," Institute for Social and Economic Research, https://mascdn.azureedge.net/cms/research_jul11_wellbeing.pdf.

2. "Does Financial Literacy Contribute to Happiness?" *The CPA Journal*, http://archives.cpajournal.com/2007/907/perspectives/p6.htm.

CHAPTER 13

1. "Most Americans Vastly Underestimate How Rich They Are Compared with the Rest of the World," *Washington Post*, https://www.washingtonpost.com/news/monkey-cage/wp/2018/08/23/most-americans-vastly-underestimate-how-rich-they-are-compared-with-the-rest-of-the-world-does-it-matter/.

2. "36% of Consumers Earning $250k+ Now Live Paycheck-to-Paycheck," PYMTS, https://www.pymnts.com/consumer-finance/2022/report-36-of-consumers-earning-250k-now-live-paycheck-to-paycheck/.

CHAPTER 17

1. Adapted from S&P Global, https://www.spglobal.com/.

2. Adapted from S&P Global, https://www.spglobal.com/.

CHAPTER 18

1. *American Journal of Epidemiology*, https://academic.oup.com/aje/article/189/11/1266/5874604.

CHAPTER 20

1. Adapted from S&P Global, https://www.spglobal.com/.
2. Adapted from S&P Global, https://www.spglobal.com/.

CHAPTER 24

1. "Trinity Study," Wikipedia, https://en.wikipedia.org/wiki/Trinity_study.

About the Author

Jason Vitug is an award-winning creator, author, speaker, entrepreneur, and producer. He is the founder of the personal finance website phroogal.com, creator of the Road to Financial Wellness, and champion of #theSmileLifestyle, a community devoted to experiential and purposeful living.

Jason is the author of the bestselling and *New York Times*–reviewed book, *You Only Live Once: The Roadmap to Financial Wellness and a Purposeful Life*. His TEDx about breaking the money taboo is one of the most viewed talks on money.

In his previous life, Jason was a nationally recognized credit union executive championing financial wellness. He currently works with Fortune 500 companies, credit unions, community banks, and fintech startups on wellness initiatives.

Jason received his bachelor's degree at Rutgers University and his MBA at Norwich University. He's an avid traveler, having been in all U.S. states, explored 45 countries, and stepped foot on 5 continents. He is also a certified yoga teacher and breathwork specialist.

Personal website: www.jasonvitug.com

Company website: www.phroogal.com

Community website: www.thesmilelifestyle.com

Acknowledgments

I'm truly blessed to be able to reach you through these pages. Writing a book is challenging but very rewarding. I've grown so much since my first book was published. And that was made possible because of your continued support.

I want to thank my community. I wouldn't be here without you. You are all unbelievably amazing, and I will continue to do my part to share ways to better your lives. I can't wait to see you in person once again.

I want to thank every person who is named in this book. I am grateful for your generosity in sharing your time and experience. Thank you to the 100 people who answered my questions about happiness and money. I've learned so much from your stories and lessons.

I want to acknowledge the thousands of people I've met in my journey: there have been so many. Understand I carry your stories with me and share them with hopes to inspire others to achieve goals and fulfill dreams. I'm positive that they surely have helped many more people.

To my editor, Kevin Harreld, and the team at Wiley for believing in this book and supporting me in creating a message of wellness and happiness in this world.

To my family and friends who continue to support my ambitions and celebrate my successes. We have all undergone many changes and tough challenges, but we continue to lift one another with love and compassion.

And to you who are reading these acknowledgments, remember this: money impacts most things, but it isn't everything. *You* are everything.

RESOURCES

To further your growth and understanding, I encourage you to use the following online resources:

Personal finance articles and financial marketplace:
www.phroogal.com

Holistic wellness resources:
www.thesmilelifestyle.com

Life lessons and wellness workshops academy:
www.thesmileuniversity.com

Index